Praise for
Reforesting Faith

"Sleeth is the perfect missionary to American evangelicals for the environmental cause."
> —ANDY CROUCH, author of *Culture Making: Recovering Our Creative Calling*

"Matthew Sleeth carries a fresh message and unique insights arising from a life of integrity and a vantage point that offers glimpses of the world that most others miss."
> —DR. JOHN STUMBO, president of the US Christian and Missionary Alliance

"*Reforesting Faith* awakens a hunger for the vastness of God as well as for the immediate presence of God. Matthew has a great gift of taking something as common as a tree and exploding the Scripture before our eyes, resulting in an overwhelming renewed love for our Lord."
> —JO ANNE LYON, general superintendent emerita of the Wesleyan Church

"Somewhere along the line, too many people picked up the notion that loving trees was somehow pagan or Druidic. As this volume makes clear, the Bible is a veritable forest, full of towering cedars and heavy-laden fruit trees."
> —BILL MCKIBBEN, author of *The Comforting Whirlwind: God, Job, and the Scale of Creation*

"Never before have I gone on a 'nature walk through the Bible,' so I'm grateful I had Matthew Sleeth as a guide. It's fascinating to see the Bible through this lens—and to realize the connection has been there all along."
> —HOWARD DAYTON, founder of Compass—Finances God's Way

"This is one of those rare books that makes you wonder how you could have read the Bible your entire life and missed so many insights and treasures. Drawing from nearly a thousand references to trees or their derivatives in the Bible, Sleeth awakens our sense of wonder and our love for the majesty of God."

—TIMOTHY C. TENNENT, PhD, president of Asbury Theological Seminary

"All of physical creation is an object lesson of spiritual truth. In this wonderful book Matthew Sleeth illuminates the most profound, prolific, and practical object in God's inventory—the tree. Both spiritual solace and spirited service find meaning in trees."

—JOEL SALATIN, farmer and author of *The Marvelous Pigness of Pigs: Respecting and Caring for All God's Creation*

"When it comes to biblical knowledge and divine insights, I can read Matthew Sleeth all day. In *Reforesting Faith* he has given us a curiosity-driven tome telling the grand story of God through the trees of Scripture."

—KYLE IDLEMAN, senior pastor of Southeast Christian Church and author of *Not a Fan: Becoming a Completely Committed Follower of Jesus* and *Don't Give Up: Faith That Gives You the Confidence to Keep Believing and the Courage to Keep Going*

"Thanks to this book, I will never look at a tree the same way again. If you care about nature at all, this is a must-read."

—ANGELA CORRELL, author of the novel *Grounded*

"Matthew Sleeth is gifted at pulling out truths in Scripture the rest of us read over. He did it with the Sabbath, and now he's done it again with trees. Read this book!"

—JESS CORRELL, chairman of First Southern National Bank and UTG Life Insurance

"Like a seasoned gallery docent, Sleeth invites us to notice the pervasive scriptural use of trees as sacramental signs in our world revealing God's presence, his activity, and his eternal purposes. The book—like its subject, the tree—is a gift, pointing us to the triune God whose daily generosity sustains us and our world."

—SHIRLEY A. MULLEN, president of Houghton College

"Matthew again connects us to the essential: God, the planet, the Sabbath, a tree. God's breath that gave life to man is being shared daily by all that breathes, including trees. This reminder brings hope and enormous joy."

—LISA RENSTROM, former president of the Sierra Club

"I never knew until reading *Reforesting Faith* how bountiful and significant trees are in God's story of the Creation, the Fall, and redemption. This book has deepened my love for God's Word and his world even more."

—KAREN SWALLOW PRIOR, author of *On Reading Well: Finding the Good Life Through Great Books* and *Fierce Convictions: The Extraordinary Life of Hannah More—Poet, Reformer, Abolitionist*

"The intrinsic and life-sustaining value of trees has long been neglected. Sleeth proves God's love for trees and draws the reader into the realization that we need to not only reforest faith but also literally reforest our forests."

—THE REV. CANON SALLY BINGHAM, founder and president emerita of Interfaith Power and Light, a religious response to climate change

"Readers of the Bible will be refreshed and quickened to see the sensible and intentional way God uses trees as blueprints for godly living and as key players in major events, including the stories of Adam and Eve,

Moses, Gideon, Jonah, and Christ. Even if you are unfamiliar with the Bible, this book will be a reminder of how important trees are to every living thing on this planet."

—GRACE JU MILLER, PHD, professor of plant biology and dean of
the School of Natural and Applied Sciences at Taylor University

"Dr. Matthew Sleeth sees biblical truths most of us who grew up in the church have overlooked. This exceptional book reflects Matthew's keen insight, his love for God's Word, and his passion for creation care."

—BOB RUSSELL, retired senior minister of Southeast Christian
Church

"Matthew Sleeth takes us on a wonderful journey along a trail of trees into a deeper and richer hope for life—*eternal life* through faith in Jesus and *thriving life* for the Father's world in which we live. This is a fun, inspirational, and provocative read."

—MARK LIEDERBACH, PHD, professor of theology, ethics,
and culture at Southeastern Baptist Theological Seminary

"*Reforesting Faith* affirms that trees play a central role in the teachings of many religions around the world. The book is a fascinating journey into our past that teaches us what we must do to ensure a future full of beauty, life, and purpose."

—DAN CHU, executive director of the Sierra Club Foundation

REFORESTING
FAITH

REFORESTING
FAITH

What Trees
Teach Us About the
Nature of God and His Love for Us

MATTHEW SLEETH, MD

WATERBROOK

All Scripture quotations, unless otherwise indicated, are taken from the Holy Bible, English Standard Version, ESV® Text Edition® (2016), copyright © 2001 by Crossway Bibles, a publishing ministry of Good News Publishers. All rights reserved. Scripture quotations marked (KJV) are taken from the King James Version. Scripture quotations marked (NIV) are taken from the Holy Bible, New International Version®, NIV®. Copyright © 1973, 1978, 1984 by Biblica Inc.® Used by permission. All rights reserved worldwide. Scripture quotations marked (NLT) are taken from the Holy Bible, New Living Translation, copyright © 1996, 2004, 2007, 2013, 2015 by Tyndale House Foundation. Used by permission of Tyndale House Publishers Inc., Carol Stream, Illinois 60188. All rights reserved. Scripture quotations marked (NRSV) are taken from the New Revised Standard Version Bible, copyright © 1989, Division of Christian Education of the National Council of the Churches of Christ in the United States of America. Used by permission. All rights reserved.

Details in some anecdotes and stories have been changed to protect the identities of the persons involved.

Hardcover ISBN 978-0-7352-9175-1
eBook ISBN 978-0-7352-9176-8

Cover design by Kelly L. Howard; cover photo by Connor Limbocker

Published in the United States by WaterBrook, an imprint of the Crown Publishing Group, a division of Penguin Random House LLC, New York.

WATERBROOK® and its deer colophon are registered trademarks of Penguin Random House LLC.

Library of Congress Cataloging-in-Publication Data
Names: Sleeth, J. Matthew, 1956–author.
Title: Reforesting faith : what trees teach us about the nature of God and his love for us / Matthew Sleeth.
Description: First edition. | Colorado Springs : WaterBrook, 2019. | Includes bibliographical references.
Identifiers: LCCN 2018037107 | ISBN 9780735291751 (hardcover) | ISBN 9780735291768 (electronic)
Subjects: LCSH: Trees in the Bible. | Bible—Criticism, interpretation, etc. | Trees—Religious aspects—Christianity. | God (Christianity)—Knowableness.
Classification: LCC BS665 .S54 2019 | DDC 220.8/58216—dc23
LC record available at https://lccn.loc.gov/2018037107

Printed in the United States of America
2019—First Edition

10 9 8 7 6 5 4 3 2 1

SPECIAL SALES
Most WaterBrook books are available at special quantity discounts when purchased in bulk by corporations, organizations, and special-interest groups. Custom imprinting or excerpting can also be done to fit special needs. For information, please email specialmarketscms@penguin randomhouse.com or call 1-800-603-7051.

To Bill and Carol Latimer,
who have planted a legacy;
To our children and grandchildren,
who need us to plant trees;
And to the One who planted all the trees,
soli Deo gloria.

 Every tree has its enemy,
few have an advocate.

—J. R. R. TOLKIEN

Contents

PART I

Laying the Groundwork

The LORD God took the man, and put him into the garden of Eden to dress it and to keep it. And the LORD God commanded the man, saying, Of every tree of the garden thou mayest freely eat: But of the tree of the knowledge of good and evil, thou shalt not eat of it: for in the day that thou eatest thereof thou shalt surely die.

—GENESIS 2:15–17, KJV

What Trees Teach Us

They are like trees
    planted by streams of water,
which yield their fruit in its season,
    and their leaves do not wither.
In all that they do, they prosper.

—PSALM 1:3, NRSV

I love trees. I always have. No one told me to love them; I just do. I love looking at them. I love sitting in their shade. I love hearing the sound of wind rustling through their leaves. But what can trees teach us? Specifically, what can trees teach us about the nature of God and his love for us?

Nearly two decades ago, during a difficult season of my life, I began to search for answers to these questions. At the time I did not believe in God. I was trained in the sciences as a physician, and my search eventually led me on a nature walk through the Bible. This book, *Reforesting Faith,* shares what I learned.

Before you embark on this trail with me, be warned: my job, my home, my family, the books I read, even the state I live in and the places I travel have all been completely changed by this journey through the woods.

God's Trees

Trees grow older, taller, and bigger than anything else on the earth. They have been with us since the beginning of time. We humans owe our very lives to the sap, bark, wood, flowers, and fruit of trees. We are their masters, yet they are our stake in the future.

And trees are beautiful. On the tops of mountains, bending over the sides of rivers, ringing the boreal latitudes, dripping wet with equatorial showers, trees blanket our world.

At night when the air is clear, trees can be seen grouped together at the edge of the forest. Illuminated in silvery moonlight, they appear to have been stopped midsentence. All night long they draw a deep breath, hold it for one count, and then from dawn to dusk exhale life-giving oxygen.

The smell of a pine forest on a hot day, the sound of palms clattering in a tropical breeze, the sight of yellow maple leaves raining down through an autumn sky—these are all evidence of trees giving praise to their Creator.

For those with ears to hear and eyes to see, the enormity of the gift of trees impresses itself upon us anew each day. Only God can make a tree.

Embarking on the Trail

Reforesting Faith is about trees in the Bible. Reading it won't make your credit card debt disappear. It won't make your teeth whiter or your hair shinier. This is not a self-help book. It's about gaining insight into why God placed our great-great-grandparents in a garden of trees and told them to dress and keep them. It will help you understand why George MacDonald, C. S. Lewis, J. R. R. Tolkien, and other great Christian writers cast the heroes of their stories as the protectors of trees and the bad guys as their enemies.

For the majority of my life, I did not believe in God. That's not the case anymore. In fact, the trees in the Bible are a crucial part of what brought me to faith.

Christianity is the only religion that weaves trees from one end of its sacred text to the other. Every important character and every major event has a tree marking the spot. There is a tree in the first and last chapter of the Bible, in the first psalm, and in the first gospel. Throughout this book we'll look at how the Bible uses trees to reveal spiritual truths about humanity and God. We'll even see how the Bible contains assertions about trees not discovered by science until the modern era.

Christians bring trees indoors once a year to celebrate the birth of their Savior. But many believe that Christians are anti-trees. Why?

This is one of the questions *Reforesting Faith* will answer. We'll go on a journey from Genesis to Revelation looking at how God uses trees in the Bible. And just like in the Bible, it's okay to skip forward to read about Jesus (in part 3) and then come back to chapter 1.

Every important character and every major event has a tree marking the spot.

Who was the first person in the Bible to plant trees? Who was the first person in Scripture to deface a tree? Why did Jesus say the kingdom of heaven is like a tree? Why are we told that trees will shout for joy when the Lord returns to judge the earth? Can trees really talk to each other the way they do in the Bible? Why do some people smile when they see a tree blowing in the breeze, while others take no notice? Which has more trees: heaven or hell? These are just a few of the questions you'll be able to answer after reading this book.

KEY TRAIL MARKERS

God's ways are made tangible in creation. Trees help us understand and see the nature and character of God. Our nature trek through the Bible will focus on several themes:

- God loves trees.
- Like God, trees are in the life business.
- Responsible stewardship is one way we can express our love and respect for God.

- Planting trees demonstrates love for our neighbors and hope for future generations.
- Trees help us regain our sense of wonder.

We are going to cover a lot of ground together. We will journey to ancient trees that stood witness to major interactions between God and our favorite Bible characters. We will also explore the varied ways God used trees to foretell the coming of the Messiah. Finally, we will see how Jesus and the apostles used the language of trees to share the good news.

Please note that in this book the term *tree* will refer not only to living trees but also to the items that come from trees, such as rods, walking sticks, staffs, wooden ladders, and the cross. We will also include parts of trees, such as fruit, seeds, roots, branches, and leaves. Further, bushes, vines, and other plants will do their part in helping us find God's deeper meaning in the context of the Bible.

Join Me on the Walk

Every time our bejeweled planet completes another circle around the sun, God gives every tree on the earth a new ring. Tick goes the clock, and another year goes by. This year will we see the trees? Will we heed the call to protect them? Will we plant the small tree today that the next generation will climb and the following one will find shade under? Will we plant in faith? Will we be called "oaks of righteousness" (Isaiah 61:3)?

Two opposing forces are at war on this planet. One says, "Look to yourself. It's all about you." The other says, "Love God, and love your neighbor." The man who said the latter claimed to be *the* true vine and the tree of life.

Reforesting Faith is about what God loves. God loves trees. Join me on a walk through the Bible and be prepared to meet the One who loves trees.

2

The Bible's Trail of Trees

The land produced vegetation—all sorts of seed-bearing plants, and trees with seed-bearing fruit. Their seeds produced plants and trees of the same kind. And God saw that it was good.

—GENESIS 1:12, NLT

Nothing beats the smell of a pine forest on a summer's day. No stillness is like the quiet of ancient redwoods at night. I can't think of a fruit grown on trees that I don't love. Trees look beautiful. They sound beautiful. They taste beautiful.

The first tree I remember was a dogwood that stood at one corner of my parents' front yard. Its limbs cascaded to the ground, forming a hidden playhouse underneath. The bark was rough, the petals silky white, and the berries red and smooth.

Perhaps if I had grown up in the desert, I would wax sentimental about cacti, but I was raised in the rural town of Woodfield,

Maryland. No hamlet ever has been more accurately christened. Woodfield was a place of forests, fertile soil, and pastures. As a youth I walked for miles along the single-lane pathways made by Holstein cows and the twin paths made by the wheels of farm vehicles. I rambled through the woods along the upper branches of the Seneca River. I lived under an open sky and a canopy created by oaks, maples, and tulip poplars. The woods came right up to the fences, which held the trees back from the rolling fields.

In kindergarten I helped plant my first tree. I poured water on the roots of a willow oak beside Woodfield Elementary School. It was the first all-electric school in America. Lady Bird Johnson came to town to admire our school and inspect our growing trees. "Anyone can plant a tree or shrub," she said, encouraging us—and the nation—to become avid tree planters. The first lady's hat and gloves and her entourage enchanted me. I still can hear how she drawled the word *shrub*, pronouncing it in a way that seemed to give it more than one syllable. I have been planting trees ever since.

In high school I was enrolled in a vocational-technical program and later worked for seven years as a carpenter. I could spot the crown in a spruce joist, the check of a pine stud, and the bow in a fir two-by-twelve. Ah, to trim out a house with clear pine, poplar, or maple. I was fortunate; construction sites were quieter back in the days before air compressors and pneumatic nail guns. We cut trim with backsaws and a hand miter box. We nailed crown molding with Blue Grass hammers. Nothing is quite as wonderful as building a house made of trees on a dry, breezy, blue autumn day.

Meeting My Better Three-Quarters

When I was in my early teens, my family seemed to implode. By the time I was sixteen, I was living on my own and working as a carpenter, and I had long since stopped going to church.

One December day when I was in my early twenties, I went to see about installing a large bay window in a periodontal surgeon's home. The family was Jewish. When their eighteen-year-old daughter walked into the room, her parents' worst nightmare began to unfold. The Jewish girl fell in love with the Gentile carpenter. Two years later Nancy and I married with a maple tree as our chuppah— the canopy we stood beneath for our vows. I brought my foot down on the glass, and we were off. *L'chaim!*

A week later I told Nancy my plan, which was to become a doctor. There was just one problem: school always had been a struggle for me. I'd never taken a class in algebra, chemistry, or biology, and I'd flunked tenth grade. Nonetheless, Nancy told me, "I'm with you—for better or worse."

I went to visit an uncle who had been a college dean. Despite my less than stellar academic record, he believed in me. "You can do this. I'll get you into the university. You have a semester, and the rest is up to you."

Fortunately, the world had changed since I'd been in high school. Though I'm extremely dyslexic, it no longer mattered that I couldn't memorize the multiplication tables. With the advent of the calculator, I could do physics. With a small dictionary ever present, I could write. I worked like a medieval alchemist on the brink of discovery. Two years and six months later, I was accepted at three medical schools.

Our son was born at the end of medical school and our daughter during my last year of residency. Afterward we moved to Maine. I worked in a hospital's emergency department. Long shifts and sleepless nights are staples of emergency medicine, but it offers priceless moments: getting hugs from children, holding hands with those who are lonely, seeing a patient get well. I especially loved suturing wounds because it gave me time to hear the stories of my patients' lives.

Nancy and I built a home in Maine, the most forest-filled state in the union. Our children went to Mast Landing School, named after the place where, four centuries earlier, towering trees emblazoned with the king's broad arrow were felled and then floated at high tide to make masts for His Majesty's ships. We planted trees along our street and a small orchard in the backyard. Life sailed along.

Then one February night, while we vacationed on an island off the southwest coast of Florida, my wife and I sat outdoors on a second-floor deck. There were no cars, roads, or people about. Our children were tucked into bed. Constellations marched above us in silence, divided by the Milky Way. A gentle wind blew over the water, and palm trees rustled in the breeze.

In the stillness Nancy turned to me and asked, "What do you think is the biggest problem on the earth?" Her question came out of nowhere, but I gave it some thought.

"The world is dying," I said. "There aren't any elms left on Elm

Street or chestnuts on Chestnut Lane. There are no caribou left in Caribou, Maine. The only buffalo left in Buffalo, New York, are the metal statues along the freeway. I don't think humanity can do business as usual for the next hundred years and expect that things are going to turn out all right."

Then Nancy asked a follow-up question: "If the world is dying, what are you going to do about it?"

I had no answer.

When My Faith in Science Failed Me

After we returned home from vacation, life stopped flowing from one good thing to another. The first of a series of tragic events occurred during our annual beach escape with my wife's side of the family. Nancy's brother was swimming in the ocean when he was pulled down by an undertow and drowned. Our kids witnessed the tragedy, and Nancy became depressed. Around the same time a mentally ill patient stalked me and was stopped only when police discovered he had murdered his mother and then hid her body in a closet.

And then came the clear September morning when I got a call from our neighbor. Her son was the same age as ours. She was calling to ask for help telling her son that his father was in the first plane that crashed into the Twin Towers.

The harder I worked to pull things together, the more our lives unraveled. The darkness would not lift. My supply of optimism ran dry.

In the hospital emergency department, I had seen plenty of bad things happen. But for the first time I woke up to the fact that evil exists in the world.

Evil is not a scientific concept; it does not lend itself to measurement. It is a spiritual concept. Up until that point I had faith only in things that could be quantified, tested, and reproduced. I didn't believe in God. If someone had pressed me about God's existence, I would have pointed to television preachers caught in scandals or the church trial of Galileo. Then I would have rested my case. When a patient would ask about my faith, I'd respond, "I believe in the healing power of third-generation antibiotics."

I'd read every book by authors such as Carl Sagan, David Attenborough, and Stephen J. Gould—all who argued for the power of science. An education in science had given me purpose, freedom, and the ability to help people. But now, with Nancy struggling and tragedy pounding at us from every side, science was failing me. What do you do when you wake up to the fact that evil is real? What do you do about a family in disarray? What do you do about a world that is dying?

Science, as powerful as it is, can't even define evil, much less distinguish between right and wrong. If I was going to find my way out of this dark place, I needed to look in places I'd never looked before. I started with some of the world's sacred texts, reading through the Ramayana and the Bhagavad Gita. Then I tackled the Koran.

One Sunday morning at the hospital, I found myself with no patients, so I went looking for something to read. On a coffee table, among back issues of *People* and *National Geographic,* I found a

Bible. I had never read one. Although we had thousands of books in our home, we didn't own a Bible. So . . . I stole it.

I started reading the book of Matthew. Within a few pages I was presented not with answers but with the Bible's great question: "What say you of Jesus?"

Right away I recognized that Jesus was unlike any person I'd ever met. He was both more human and more godly than anyone I'd known. Although my coming to faith was a process—more like Peter's than Paul's—it soon began transforming every area of my life.

Over the next two years, my son, then my wife, and then my daughter came to believe, as I did, in Jesus as their savior. Jesus does not claim to be a good teacher or a moral leader—although I think anyone with even a passing knowledge of him will allow that he is both. He boldly and unequivocally claims to be the Son of God, saying, "If you've seen me, you've seen God" (see John 14:9). If his assertion is not true, then Jesus is a liar. On the other hand, if Jesus is who he says he is, then he is Lord of all creation. There is no middle ground. We are given only these two choices. My family chose to believe him, to trust him, and to follow him.

What God Thinks About Trees

The two years following my conversion to Christianity were not easy. I had been practicing medicine for fifteen years. But I finally answered Nancy's second question from our trip to Florida: "What are you going to do about a world that's dying?" I told her I wanted to quit my job as chief of staff and head of the emergency department and spend the rest of my life serving God and helping to save the planet. Concerned about putting food on the table, let alone paying for college for our two teenage kids, Nancy replied, "Honey, are you sure we need to do that much?"

We sold our home, gave away half our possessions, and moved to a house the size of our former garage. Soon after, we started going to a church where the congregation became like family and remain so to this day. The debt of gratitude we owe them is incalculable. The church is a conservative one. It believes that Scripture is the inspired, inerrant Word of God. That's why we went there. But when I volunteered to plant trees around the church's grounds, one of the pastors said I had the theology of a tree hugger. This was not meant as a compliment. My first reaction to the pastor's comment was, "Maybe I'm wrong. Maybe God doesn't care about trees."

God has an astounding fondness for trees.

Back then our whole family was new to Christianity. My daughter hadn't yet married a pastor. My son wasn't a missionary pediatrician in Africa, and I'd yet to write books on applied theology or preach at more than a thousand colleges and churches around the world. What did I know about the theology of trees?

But ever since I encountered the gospel for the first time in my forties, the Bible has been my compass. So when I was called a tree hugger, I turned to Scripture to get my bearings. I read from Genesis to Revelation, underlining everything the Bible has to say about trees. And here's what I found: God has an astounding fondness for trees.

GOD'S TRAIL OF TREES

Other than God and people, the Bible mentions trees more than any other living thing. There is a tree on the first page of Genesis, in the first psalm, on the first page of the New Testament, and on the last page of Revelation. Every significant theological event in the Bible is marked by a tree. Whether it is the Fall, the Flood, or the overthrow of Pharaoh, every major event in the Bible has a tree, branch, fruit, seed, or some part of a tree marking the spot.

Jesus said, "I am the true vine, and my Father is the vinedresser" (John 15:1). The wisdom of the Bible is a tree of life (Proverbs 3:18). We are told to be "like trees planted by streams of water, which yield their fruit in its season" (Psalm 1:3, NRSV).

Moreover, every major character in the Bible appears in conjunction with a tree. In the Old Testament, Noah received the olive leaf (Genesis 8:11), Abraham sat under "the oaks of Mamre" (18:1), and Moses stood barefoot in front of the burning bush (Exodus 3:2–5). At first glance Joseph might appear to be an exception, but the Bible tells us that Joseph simply *is* a tree (Genesis 49:22).

The same pattern holds true in the New Testament. Think of Zacchaeus climbing the sycamore fig (Luke 19:1–4), the blind man seeing people as if they were trees walking (Mark 8:24), and the disciples gathering on the Mount of Olives (Luke 22:39). The apostle Paul asserted that if we have gone for a walk in the woods, we are without excuse for knowing God (Romans 1:20). Paul also wrote that Christians are like branches grafted into Israel's tree trunk, with roots that help us stand fast and firm no matter what troubles come our way (11:17–18).

Jesus himself declared that the kingdom of heaven is like a tree (Matthew 13:31–32). The only thing that Jesus ever harmed was a

Other than God and people, the Bible mentions trees more than any other living thing.

tree (Mark 11:12–14, 20–21), and the only thing that could harm him was a tree. After Jesus was resurrected, he was mistaken for a gardener (John 20:15). This was not a mistake. Jesus is the new Adam who has come to redeem all

of creation. Heaven is a place where the leaves of a tree heal all the nations (Revelation 22:1–2). As if to underscore this forest of metaphors, Jesus's last "I am" statement is "I am the root and the descendant of David" (Revelation 22:16).

From Genesis to Revelation God has blazed a trail of trees through the Bible. The reason so many people love trees is because we are created in God's image. God loves trees, and so should we.

Missing the Trees for the Forest

God put all these trees in the Bible for a reason. He had a world of symbols to choose from, but God decided to use trees to tell the gospel. So why have most people never heard a sermon on trees?

I began a decadelong process of inquiry and research, starting with the oldest Bible on my shelf. It's a King James study Bible published more than a century ago. The commentary section includes twenty pages on trees and plants, with more than fifty illustrations and four full-page pictures of famous trees in the Bible. All these references and illustrations indicate what the editors in the nineteenth century felt was a balanced approach to studying Scripture.

In contrast, the 2013 edition of the *King James Study Bible* by the same publishing house has not a single page of commentary on trees or plants. The index contains only three tree entries. While minimal, this is better than some other modern study Bibles, which contain none.

In the 1611 King James Version of the Bible, the words *tree, leaf, branch, root, fruit,* and *seed* occur 967 times. This tally doesn't include specific tree names, such as palms, terebinths, figs, oaks, sycamores, acacias, willows, brooms, and tamarisks.

A quick look at three modern English translations shows that the same six tree-related words appear hundreds of times less frequently. The tally is 230 fewer times in the English Standard Version (ESV); 267 fewer times in the New International Version (NIV); and 274 fewer times in the New Living Translation (NLT).

Despite trees serving as God's favorite metaphor in Scripture, most people today have never heard a sermon on trees in the Bible. This was not always the case. We have a long history of writers who understood the connection between trees and God. If we reach back more than a thousand years to one of the oldest works of English literature, "The Dream of the Rood," we hear the story of the Crucifixion told from the tree's point of view.

A glance at a few of Charles Spurgeon's sermon titles indicates what people were hearing from the pulpit during the mid- to late

1800s. His sermons included "Christ the Tree of Life," "The Trees in God's Court," "The Cedars of Lebanon," "The Apple Tree in the Woods," "The Beauty of the Olive Tree," "The Sound in the Mulberry Trees," and "The Leafless Tree." Spurgeon, the "prince of preachers," had no difficulty seeing both the trees *and* the forest in Scripture.

More recently George MacDonald, J. R. R. Tolkien, and C. S. Lewis—three of the most beloved and influential Christian fiction writers of all time—championed trees. Whether it is MacDonald's picture of heaven in *At the Back of the North Wind,* Tolkien's tree haven Lothlórien in Middle-earth, or the way trees respond when Aslan is on the move in Lewis's Chronicles of Narnia, each author paints a picture of shalom among the trees. The good guys live under, in, and around trees. They value, protect, and even talk to trees. In contrast, the bad guys, such as Lewis's Tash and Tolkien's Sauron, are clear-cutters of trees—even talking trees!

A number of factors point to why trees have gone missing from our faith. But lying at the heart of the explanation is the resurgence of a first-century heresy called dualism. Dualism calls God's creation evil, assigning merit only to things of the Spirit. Of course, no part of the Bible supports this heresy. And the incarnation of God as a man named Jesus clearly is at odds with this false dichotomy.

The logical conclusion of dualism is that God made himself corrupt simply by taking on the form of matter—human flesh. This leads us to another first-century heresy called docetism—but I digress. One does not have to be a systematic theologian to ask this: "If the spiritual is superior to the material, why did God love the earth so much that he sent his only Son to save it?" The most dangerous consequence of this heresy is that it prevents us from hearing God speak to us through our everyday interactions with his creation.

 Trees are not randomly placed in Scripture. They mark the most important events, including the Creation, the Fall, the Crucifixion, and the Resurrection. This is not a coincidence. The Bible is one interwoven book, written by one God.

In fact, if I had to pick one subject other than Jesus to corroborate the inspired origin of the Bible, I'd pick trees. Why? Because while the Bible was written by many people over many centuries, the consistent use of trees points to one Author.

Trees are not randomly placed in Scripture. They mark the most important events, including the Creation, the Fall, the Crucifixion, and the Resurrection. This is not a coincidence. The Bible is one interwoven book, written by one God.

I love trees. God loves trees. Let's go walking through the Bible looking for trees. Maybe we'll catch a glimpse of the Gardener himself.

3

The Fruit That Changed Everything

The LORD God planted a garden in Eden, in the east;
and there he put the man whom he had formed. Out of
the ground the LORD God made to grow every tree that
is pleasant to the sight and good for food, the tree of life
also in the midst of the garden, and the tree of the
knowledge of good and evil.

—GENESIS 2:8–9, NRSV

All available scientific evidence points to life being extraordinarily rare in the universe. Suns, planets, black matter, and empty space are common, but life is precious. In our solar system alone, the odds of being an atom in a living thing are incalculably small—something on the order of one in 3,500 trillion. As we push beyond our solar system deeper into space, the odds drop dramatically.

Life is so abundant on the earth that we take it for granted. It's in the frozen tundra, in deep caves, above the tree line, under the ocean, beneath our fingernails—everywhere.

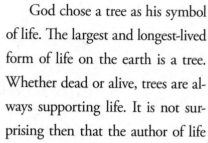

The largest and longest-lived form of life on the earth is a tree.

God chose a tree as his symbol of life. The largest and longest-lived form of life on the earth is a tree. Whether dead or alive, trees are always supporting life. It is not surprising then that the author of life would put a tree at the beginning, middle, and end of his message to us, the Bible.

The Edge of the Forest

Genesis 1:11 marks both the third day of creation and a triumph for chlorophyll. From this point on in the Bible, whether it is a microscopic phytoplankton or a giant sequoia, trees stand as the Bible's symbol of the plant kingdom. The writers of Scripture often used one noun to stand for a number of related nouns. For instance, the word *cattle* can refer to cows, but it also can stand for all domesticated beasts.

Here is a simple way to see the abundance of trees in Scripture. If you have a Bible and a pen or marker, you can do this exercise. Beginning with Genesis 1:11, highlight every sentence in the first three chapters that contains a reference to a tree (or part of a tree, such as a seed or fruit) until you reach the sword-wielding cherubim guarding the tree in the last sentence of Genesis 3.

Now take a glance at your work. Nearly one-third of the sentences in the first three chapters of the Bible contain a tree. One-third. Skim over your highlighting and you'll see a forest beginning to emerge.

A God-Sized View of Time

On the third day of creation, we find the beginning of the Bible's forest. Before we go further, let me acknowledge that some readers take the time intervals in Genesis literally, while others do not. For thousands of years people have read the opening chapters of Genesis to find answers to spiritual questions. Sixteen hundred years ago Saint Augustine warned Christians not to use Genesis as a science textbook. I do not wish to go against his counsel.

Nonetheless, we need to establish parameters around Bible passages we consider metaphor and content we take literally. When Jesus promised that if we have the faith of a mustard seed we could move mountains (Matthew 17:20), he was not saying people could levitate Mount Sinai.

Earnest readers of the Bible have long debated whether "the evening and the morning" referred to in Genesis stands for a twenty-four-hour day, a seven-day week, or a billion years. Some read Genesis and understand that the Bible teaches that the universe was created in seven days, and of course they are right. Other equally earnest readers point to Genesis 2:4: "These are the generations of the heavens and the earth when they were created, in the day that the LORD God made the earth and the heavens." Such readers believe this allows for either a vast timescale or an instantaneous one. Their argument is equally valid and biblically grounded. Which view is correct? Was everything created in a week, a day, or a generation?

It is helpful to note how theologians of old resolved this paradox. "God," they reasoned, "doesn't experience time as we do." As proof they pointed to lines of Scripture such as, "With the Lord one day is as a thousand years, and a thousand years as one day" (2 Peter 3:8).

Trees point toward who God is, who we are, how the world works, and why evil exists.

"God," they postulated, "lives outside of time."

To those who demanded reproducible proof, this must have seemed like nonsense. People may *perceive* time differently, but time moves in one direction, at a uniform speed, and no one has ever observed differently. But at the dawn of the twentieth century, Edwin Hubble and Albert Einstein came along and said, "Not so fast . . ."

I believe that once there was nothing and then God spoke everything into existence. Whether this happened in a week or over eons I leave up to you. In my discussion of Genesis, I'll use the language of one week. Feel free to substitute generations or a day as you see fit.

The goal of this book is not to identify the age of rocks but to find out why the Rock of Ages planted so many trees in the Bible. We know this much: trees point toward who God is, who we are, how the world works, and why evil exists.

TREES MAKE GOD'S WAYS TANGIBLE

God devoted a considerable amount of biblical real estate to trees. Let's look at the third day of creation to see where this all starts.

> God said, Let the earth bring forth grass, the herb yielding
> seed, and the fruit tree yielding fruit after his kind, whose
> seed is in itself, upon the earth: and it was so. And the earth
> brought forth grass, and herb yielding seed after his kind, and
> the tree yielding fruit, whose seed was in itself, after his kind:
> and God saw that it was good. (Genesis 1:11–12, KJV)

Botanists who read these lines will pick up on the two broad categories of plants. The first are gymnosperms. As applied to trees, gymnosperms represent conifers (or softwoods) such as pines, yews, cedars, and redwoods. These trees make seeds, but the seeds are not contained within fruit. The second category, angiosperms—from the Greek *angion,* which means "container"—bear fruit that contain the plant's seeds. This class of tree is represented by hardwoods, or deciduous trees, such as peaches, pears, oaks, and ash.

Throughout the Bible (just as in biology classes today), the categorization of trees into fruit-bearing and non-fruit-bearing is maintained. This distinction is upheld in the Old Testament, and later we'll see that Christ was well aware of it too.

Let's begin by exploring some of the tree-related references we highlighted in the first two chapters of Genesis:

God said, Behold, I have given you every herb bearing seed, which is upon the face of all the earth, and every tree, in the which is the fruit of a tree yielding seed; to you it shall be for meat. And to every beast of the earth, and to every fowl of the air, and to every thing that creepeth upon the earth, wherein there is life, I have given every green herb for meat: and it was so. And God saw every thing that he had made, and, behold, it was very good. And the evening and the morning were the sixth day. (1:29–31, KJV)

The LORD God formed man of the dust of the ground, and breathed into his nostrils the breath of life; and man became a living soul. And the LORD God planted a garden eastward in Eden; and there he put the man whom he had formed. And out of the ground made the LORD God to grow every tree that is pleasant to the sight, and good for food; the tree of life also in the midst of the garden, and the tree of knowledge of good and evil. (2:7–9, KJV)

The LORD God took the man, and put him into the garden of Eden to dress it and to keep it. And the LORD God commanded the man, saying, Of every tree of the garden thou mayest freely eat: But of the tree of the knowledge of good and evil, thou shalt not eat of it: for in the day that thou eatest thereof thou shalt surely die. (2:15–17, KJV)

Here are attributes God assigned to trees in the verses we just looked at:

- Trees/chlorophyll provide all the energy for animals (1:29–30).
- God planted a garden filled with trees as a place in which humans could live (2:8).
- Trees are "pleasant to the sight" (2:9).
- The tree of life is a symbol of human access to God (2:9).
- Humanity's first job was to dress (take care of) and keep (preserve) the trees (2:15).
- Humanity is given moral agency through the tree of the knowledge of good and evil (2:16).

Within the first two chapters of the Bible, life, death, human agency, respiration, food, aesthetics, human purpose, and a connection to God all are tied to trees. The link between plants and animals isn't just an academic curiosity; it is an inescapable fact of life. Without humans, trees would manage just fine. Without trees, people would perish. Everything on the earth that moves uses energy that is stored in bonds between carbon atoms, first formed in a green plant through the process of photosynthesis. You, me, earthworms, ants, bees, tigers, sloths, and aphids: we all run on trees. And it's not just that we use plant energy (calories) to power our brains and bodies. We need the oxygen from trees to burn this fuel. The tree of life is aptly named on every level.

> Without humans, trees would manage just fine. Without trees, people would perish.

Trees Keep the Air On

Trees take carbon dioxide molecules from the air and knit them together with water using the sun's energy. The products of this process are oxygen and sugar. We inhale the trees' oxygen and use it to burn the trees' sugars for energy. Then we exhale carbon dioxide. Ever since God jump-started the cycle by blowing life into Adam's nostrils, nothing has changed. Today, we may have more detailed explanations of the carbon cycle than the one summarized in Genesis, but none are more elegant or equally prescient.

The Bible uses only 282 Hebrew words to describe all of creation. It doesn't mention nuclear weak or strong bonds. It doesn't mention gravity or electromagnetic forces. It doesn't specify how many electrons are in the outer shell of carbon atoms. But it does tell us where all the energy to run everything that creeps, crawls, and runs comes from, and it points like an arrow to the source of oxygen.

We take for granted that oxygen comes from trees, but the link isn't intuitive. Many of history's greatest minds didn't know what a fifth grader does today. Isaac Newton, Leonardo da Vinci, and Johannes Kepler might have laughed if a child had told them that trees were powering every moving thing. For almost all of human history, we didn't have a clue that we were breathing trees.

Scientists have long pondered where the atmosphere came from and what it is in air that makes life possible. One of the prevailing theories was that air came from rocks. If you've ever seen mist rising off a sunlit cliff face in the morning, you'll understand where this theory originated. Not until the 1770s was the link between trees and breathing discovered. Scientists found that a mouse in a sealed jar with plants inside and placed in the sunlight was a happy mouse. They also found that the mouse died if either the sun or the plants were taken away. The sun-plant-animal oxygen connection was discovered.

Biblically, this dependence was foreshadowed when God blew the breath of life into Adam's nostrils and in the next motion pivoted and planted trees. At the level of respiration, humans and trees share an eerily similar architecture. This similarity wasn't established until the age of plastics, which allowed anatomists to make a cast of the tubes leading into a human lung. A bronchogram, or a cast, of our respiratory "tree" is indistinguishable from the shape of a bare oak tree.

A bronchogram, which beautifully
demonstrates the trees we carry inside us

The Tree Aesthetic

Genesis 2:7 states, "The LORD God formed man of the dust of the ground" (KJV). It's estimated that all the carbon, iron, calcium, and other elements necessary to make a human would cost $4.50 if ordered from a chemical supply house. The image of God's forming Adam from the dust is not only poetic but also accurate: humans are dirt cheap. The value of a human, however, is not derived from the elements we're made of. We are jars of clay containing something priceless. It's the initial breath from God that makes the difference.

In Genesis 2:8 we learn that "God planted a garden eastward in Eden; and there he put the man whom he had formed" (KJV). God is everywhere, but it seems he is easier to find near trees. The Bible states that no one can earn his way to heaven. We are saved by God's grace alone (Ephesians 2:8–9). Yet if God made an exception to this rule, I think it might be for gardeners.

Trees have a way of bridging generations, connecting us with the past and inviting us to dream of the future. When we plant and tend trees, we imitate God.

I live in Lexington, Kentucky, a few blocks from the edge of Ashland Park, a six-hundred-acre neighborhood of meandering tree-lined streets designed a century ago by the Olmsted brothers. Although the brothers are best known for their design of Central Park in New York City, the Olmsteds planned many parks and neighborhoods across America.

My wife and I walk daily in the neighborhood they designed. We pass underneath towering oaks, ginkgoes, and sycamores. I can't help but feel a debt to them. Trees have a way of bridging generations, connecting us with the past and inviting us to dream of the future. When we plant and tend trees, we imitate God.

Genesis 2:8–9 states that God placed the first human in a garden, and then God planted "every tree that is pleasant to the sight." If you are new to the Bible, this phrase may not seem unusual. But it is without parallel. It represents God's weighing in on the issue of beauty. If you like the looks of trees, you're not alone. You share your aesthetic with God.

Not surprisingly, when God gave directions for building his tabernacle and his temple, he loaded up the blueprints with trees. The ark, the table, the temple cornices, and the priest's staff all were made of trees. If something was made of gold, such as the lampstands, it was crafted to resemble a tree. God even specified that the high priest's robe end in a tree bauble—a pomegranate.

Two Trees in Paradise

God planted two special trees in the middle of Eden: the tree of life and the tree of the knowledge of good and evil. You take a significant theological risk if you overlook or undervalue these trees. They are two of the most important trees in the Bible. The tree of life stands for all life created by God, and he declared it "good." It is a tree of justice, beauty, truth, love, light, and righteousness. While in the garden, Adam and Eve ate freely from the tree of life. To eat from, be grafted into, or take hold of this tree is to obtain everlasting life. Thus, by definition, the tree of life stands for Christ. The rest of the Bible—and this book—centers on the tree of life.

The other tree planted in the middle of paradise was the tree of the knowledge of good and evil. This tree opens the door to pride, evil, greed, arrogance, hatred, cruelty, malice, ugliness, and callousness. To eat from this tree is bad, while to consciously avoid this tree is good. The tree of the knowledge of good and evil symbolizes death, and death is bad.

So why is this tree called the tree of the knowledge of good *and* evil? Why include the word *good* in the name? I believe it's to underscore the fact that evil exists in contrast to good. All sin is really a perversion of something good. In the language of today, we might just as easily have called it the tree of right and wrong.

God put the poisonous tree in the middle of the garden, where Adam and Eve couldn't mistake it. "This tree will kill you the minute you eat from it," God warned. He then offered some helpful advice: "The tree of life is always here right beside temptation—just to remind you." Beside every bad decision in life, there is a good alternative.

God saw that it was not good for man to be alone, so God made woman and brought her to man. Naked and unashamed, they were instructed to "dress" and "keep" the garden (Genesis 2:15, KJV). The

Bible gives no details about their honeymoon. It preserves the mysteries of their marriage until the day everything went wrong. On that day evil, in the character of a serpent, entered the garden, and the Fall happened.

> When the woman saw that the tree was good for food, and that it was pleasant to the eyes, and a tree to be desired to make one wise, she took of the fruit thereof, and did eat, and gave also unto her husband with her; and he did eat. And the eyes of them both were opened, and they knew that they were naked; and they sewed fig leaves together, and made themselves aprons. And they heard the voice of the LORD God walking in the garden in the cool of the day: and Adam and his wife hid themselves from the presence of the LORD God amongst the trees of the garden. And the LORD God called unto Adam, and said unto him, Where art thou? (Genesis 3:6–9, KJV)

The Bible doesn't specify what kind of fruit Adam and Eve ate. Paintings often depict her reaching for an apple. Interestingly, the Latin word for "apple," *malum,* is also the Latin word for "evil." The fruit of the tree of the knowledge of good and evil appealed to three of Eve's appetites: her palate, her eye, and her ego. Would you have eaten the fruit if you'd been in her place? I would have. Most of us succumb to a temptation even if it promises only one of the three cravings Eve thought she was going to satisfy.

The First Sin

Can you recall the circumstances surrounding the first time you knowingly sinned? Do you remember your own fall? Did something appeal to your appetite or your ego? Did something catch your eye? Did someone talk you into it?

The first time I consciously decided to sin was in the Ben Franklin five-and-dime store. As I stood facing hundreds of penny candies corralled in neat glass partitions, it was as if a snake slithered across the red and green linoleum tiles and whispered, "Did your parents really say you can't have one of these?"

I was a pretty good kid. I held out three, maybe four seconds. Then I stole a piece of candy and hid it in my pocket.

The little candy named after a nuclear explosion didn't offer me the power to become a god. It wasn't a thing of beauty. All it offered was a taste of the forbidden. I stole it, and I got away with it. Half a century later, however, I can still feel the heat from that Atomic Fireball. I sinned, and it was only the beginning.

Stealing and eating something forbidden was my first sin. Was it yours? Or was it lying to your mom? Or hitting your sibling?

How did Adam and Eve react when they were caught? The same way you and I did the first time we were caught: with a lie or a cover-up or a denial. The lamest excuse of all is to blame someone else.

Before the Fall, God, Adam, and Eve met up on a regular basis. But not on the day of the Fall. That's the day they stood him up. For the first time, we no longer sought God; God had to come looking for us (Romans 3:11). God knew what they had done, so he called out, "Where are you?" The day before, Adam and Eve had been naked and unashamed while they went about their calling of protecting paradise. Now they hid behind fig leaves they had stripped from the trees they were charged with dressing. Talk about walking off the job. As they heard God approach, they cowered behind the trees of the garden.

The warning "In the day that thou eatest thereof thou shalt surely die" (Genesis 2:17, KJV) must have run through their minds as they straightened their makeshift clothing with sticky hands. Did they die that day? No, they did not. Not all things in the Bible are literal. Some have deeper meanings. Adam and Eve lived long lives. On the day of the Fall, their death was not physical, although that began too. The death they suffered was a spiritual one. They were separated from God. Their walk in the park was over.

The next scene in the Bible is almost too painful to read. God declared that childbirth would be dangerous and would hurt. Eve and Adam would need each other, and they would argue. Adam would work the ground, but it would never be easy. The ground would yield thorns and thistles. Together the couple would no longer have access to the tree of life, meaning they would age and then die. And as if that weren't enough, they would be evicted from paradise.

Do you think God was too harsh? What would you do if someone took a wrecking ball to paradise? Adam and Eve lived long lives compared to us, but why did they have to grow old and die? Was God too exacting, or do you feel that they got off lightly?

In one sense, mortality was a blessing rather than a curse. Can you imagine being born on a planet where fallen humanity lived forever? Today, the eight wealthiest people on the earth have more money than the least wealthy 3.6 *billion* put together.[1] Human greed knows no limits, so God gave us an inescapable one: death. Greed is only one of our faults. Think about our lust for power. Can you imagine if the likes of Nebuchadnezzar, Alexander the Great, and Genghis Khan were still on the earth and had multiple lifetimes to spend grabbing power? You and I wouldn't stand a snowball's chance in a microwave.

The Fall Is Real

When sin entered the world, it affected all of creation, not just humanity. Every time we clear-cut a forest or destroy a species, we continue the legacy of the Fall. Long before Europeans came to America, the native population killed off sloths, camels, and other species. Later, when Europeans arrived, the curse on the land kicked into high gear. Only a few hundred years after Europeans landed on the shores of the New World, the most prolific bird species in North America—passenger pigeons—became extinct. The most common commercial fish from the Great Lakes—blue pike—were gone. The most abundant species of tree in the eastern United States—the American chestnut—went missing. These are not obscure examples; they represent some of the most important species to inhabit North America, and North America is not unique. Every continent has a similar story. From the perspective of the earth, the results of the Fall are all too real.

THE BIBLE'S WISDOM
IS A TREE OF LIFE

We have only dipped our toes into the first three chapters of the Bible, yet we see that God places the most important events under, around, on, and next to trees.

Thus far, we've seen Satan successfully tempt Adam and Eve. We've seen fig leaves used in an attempt to hide human shame, the earth grow thorns and thistles, the tree of life taken away, and the gates of paradise locked. We've seen humanity lose its innocence and fail to regain its righteousness. But don't despair: while brutally honest, the Bible is a story of hope and redemption.

There's something I've learned about reading the Bible: if you start with the premise that the book is true, it will reward you. Only a dullard begins a story by interrupting the narrator. Something miraculous takes place when you approach this book in faith. That doesn't mean you have to understand or like everything you read in it. When I don't understand 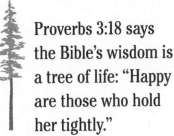 Proverbs 3:18 says the Bible's wisdom is a tree of life: "Happy are those who hold her tightly." something, I put a mental sticky note (or an actual one) on that passage and ask the Lord to reveal its meaning.

At times I have waited a decade, but I've gotten answers. I'm still waiting for others. After you've had dozens of questions answered, you begin to realize that the Bible is all about seeking truth, finding the answers, and having the truths change the course of your life. Proverbs 3:18 says the Bible's wisdom is a tree of life: "Happy are those who hold her tightly" (NLT). The first psalm says those who pursue the Bible's wisdom eventually become like fruit-bearing trees, growing leaves that never wither (verse 3).

PART II

Seeds of Faith

The righteous flourish like the palm tree
    and grow like a cedar in Lebanon.
They are planted in the house of the Lord;
    they flourish in the courts of our God.
They still bear fruit in old age;
    they are ever full of sap and green.

—Psalm 92:12–14

4

The Tree of Hospitality

Reading about nature is fine, but if a person walks in the woods and listens carefully, he can learn more than what is in books, for they speak with the voice of God.

—GEORGE WASHINGTON CARVER

Ours is a moviegoing age. We understand the unspoken language of films. Because of this shared understanding, directors can foreshadow events without using dialogue.

Consider an attractive, unattached man and woman who have a disagreement every time their paths cross. The odds of them falling in love seem little better than zero. But when violins begin playing softly in the background, the odds soar to nearly 100 percent. The audience sees the first kiss coming because we are privy to music the characters can't hear.

Directors, however, aren't limited to foreshadowing romance. Picture a young woman home alone one night. We see her doing mundane things: reading a book, washing dishes. Everything is peaceful. But what message is communicated when violins start bowing short strokes high on the E string? *EEee EEee EEee.* Even though the on-screen character goes about her business unaware of impending danger, we tense as she heads down to the basement, walks up the dark attic stairs, or turns on the shower. "Get out of the house!" we want to shout.

When you see a tree, branch, bush, root, or fruit on the page, look for God.

In much the same way that movies employ music to help tell a story, the Bible uses trees. A tree marks every important event in Scripture. But just as characters in a movie can't hear the background music, it seems that biblical characters are not aware of the significance of the trees they stand beside.

Trees are always included for a reason. Thousands of years after the stories in the Bible were written, God is still using trees to help us understand what's going on. When you spot a tree in the Bible, you can be confident that heaven is on the way—even though the character in Scripture may have no idea. When you see a tree, branch, bush, root, or fruit on the page, look for God.

THE APPLE HASN'T ROLLED FAR

After Adam and Eve were cast from paradise, they raised a son named Cain and another named Abel. When Cain and Abel brought offerings to God, the Lord approved of Abel's gift but not Cain's. Is this because Abel brought meat and Cain brought vegetables? Although some have made much of the gifts themselves, I don't think the nature of the two gifts influenced God's approval or disapproval.

In one sense anything we give to God is like offering the owner of the beach a grain of sand. God's approval is based on the spirit in which a gift is given. One of God's all-time favorite gifts was the offering of two coins given by a poor widow (Mark 12:41–44). Like the widow's offering, Abel's gift was an offering from the heart given in joy. Cain's, in contrast, was given reluctantly, out of a sense of obligation. The Lord told Cain that if his attitude were to improve, his gifts would be approved. However, God warned, if Cain were to let his anger go unchecked, sin would be found waiting for him. In the end, Cain murdered his brother (Genesis 4:6–8).

Cain's killing Abel is not the first crime recorded in the Bible, but it is the first murder. The killing of Abel by his big brother puts to rest any notion that if God had overlooked Adam and Eve's sin, things might have gone back to normal.

If we examine our own histories, we'll find that the apple has not rolled far from the tree. Have you ever caught a glimpse of Cain in the mirror when you are brushing your teeth, shaving, or putting on makeup? How about when a friend gets an award or promotion and you don't? Do you rejoice for your friend, or do you feel jealous? Any sibling rivalry?

AN ARK MADE FROM GOPHER WOOD

Cain's killing Abel was only the beginning of humanity's slide to the bottom. Civilization was up to no good in a hurry. In short order we were far from God's image bearers. God finally said, "Enough!" "God saw that the wickedness of man was great in the earth, and that every imagination of the thoughts of his heart was only evil continually" (Genesis 6:5, KJV).

God decided to hit the reset button by flooding the earth. The account of the deluge can be read in Genesis 6–9. Noah alone was upright and righteous in the sight of the Lord, so God picked Noah to lead a rescue mission.

The tree marking this event is the gopher tree. *Gopher* is simply the transliteration of the Hebrew word for the tree Noah used to build the ark. I don't think it's a coincidence that no one knows the exact species of gopher trees. God promised we'd never need it again. This was not the last time, however, that God would use a tree to save humanity (Hebrews 2:14–15).

The gopher tree has a lesson for us today: obey the Lord even if you're the only one doing it.

The gopher tree has a lesson for us today: obey the Lord even if you're the only one doing it. For Noah this meant building a boat where there was no water. Noah was the first follower of God in a line that led to the likes of William Wilberforce, Dietrich Bonhoeffer, and Corrie ten Boom—believers who went against the grain to follow God.

Our society often venerates individuality at the same time it encourages conformity. But according to the Bible, neither individuality nor conformity is a virtue. Obeying God is the virtue. Sometimes this leads one to clear conformity and other times to apparent individualism. True believers are simply following God. The less the world conforms to the words and the ways of God, the more followers of God find themselves isolated and unpopular. If you seek the Lord's face, you will inevitably find yourself outnumbered.

An Olive Branch

Noah landed the ark as the floodwaters receded. It wasn't long before three symbols appeared: a dove, a rainbow, and an olive leaf (Genesis 8:11; 9:12–16). The dove is the symbol of God's Holy Spirit. Doves appear thirty-one times in Scripture and are associated with purity and sacrifice. The Holy Spirit appeared descending "like a dove" as Jesus began his ministry (Luke 3:22). If you see a dove in a religious painting, the artist is likely representing the presence of the Holy Spirit.

The rainbow is the sign of a covenant between God, humans, and animals. It's God's sticky note in the sky to himself: "Don't flood the world again, no matter how far off the rails humans go." A rainbow comprises the visible light spectrum—the electromagnetic waves between infrared and ultraviolet. A rainbow is not only a symbol; it is literally the entire bandwidth of light that a human eye can see. As such, a rainbow is the perfect symbol for God the Father. Look for a rainbow at the top of many religious paintings from the Middle Ages through the Renaissance; they are the artist's shorthand for God.

Anytime something appears for the first or last time in Scripture, we should take special note. The rainbow appears in both the first and the last book of the Bible (Genesis and Revelation). Revelation 4:3, written by the apostle John two thousand years ago, describes the rainbow as a circle of light surrounding the throne of God. But aren't rainbows half circles, not full circles? From the viewpoint of humans standing on the ground, yes. But with the advent of flight in the last few generations, we can now see the full circle of a rainbow. While the Bible is not meant to be a science textbook, I find examples such as this one reassuring. A rainbow is all the light we can see symbolizing a God we cannot see.

Finally, let's consider the olive leaf. The leaf delivered by a dove was from a very specific species of tree belonging to the Oleaceae family. The ancient world relied on this tree for its nutritious fruit, but the industrialized Western world rediscovered its benefits only recently. The ancient world also used olive oil for another purpose: anointing members of royalty.

One of the names for Jesus is the *Christ,* which means "the Anointed One." Jesus called himself "the true vine" (John 15:1). No named tree is more closely associated with the life and ministry of Christ than the olive tree. When Jesus spent his last moments of freedom in a late-night prayer to his Father, he asked his disciples to stay with him. They fell asleep, but the olive trees never deserted him.

The dove, rainbow, and olive leaf represent the Trinity: God the Holy Spirit, God the Father, and God the Son.

I'd like to tell you that after the Flood, Noah and his family started fresh and that Noah or one of his sons became the Son of Man who put things right. But alas, this did not happen. Noah got drunk, and his son Ham acted shamefully when Noah passed out.

As a result, Noah cursed the descendants of Ham—the Canaanites. He blessed his other two sons (Genesis 9:18–27). Then things continued downhill. Fast-forward to Abraham—or Abram, as he originally was named. The story of Abraham is closely associated with an oak tree. This is one of the most famous trees in human history.

ABRAHAM'S OAK

In Genesis 12 God called Abram to leave his home and travel to an unknown land. Then, in Genesis 17:4–5, God said to him, "Behold, my covenant is with you, and you shall be the father of a multitude of nations. No longer shall your name be called Abram, but your name shall be Abraham."

God also changed Sarai's name to Sarah and promised her a son, although she was nearly ninety years old. Through Abraham (which translates to "father of many") and Sarah, all the nations of the earth would be blessed. Abraham and Sarah were to become the great-great-great-grandparents of Jesus. Their line culminates in the Messiah.

Let's journey back thousands of years ago to a dry, hot day and imagine the scene that began in Genesis 18: Abraham was dozing against the door of his tent pitched in the shade of a spreading oak. It was the middle of the day, and heat waves shimmered off the surrounding hills. His eighty-nine-year-old wife, a decade his junior, was taking a nap in the tent. Cattle and sheep lay underneath every tree and bush. Two tethered donkeys swished flies from each other's faces as they stood head to tail.

Hoary-headed Abraham opened his eyes, squinted, and saw three strangers approaching the camp.

The book of Hebrews tells us that Abraham did not realize the strangers were anything other than men. Despite this, he and Sarah treated the visitors with the utmost grace and hospitality. Abraham offered them his seat. He brought water to wash their feet. Sarah fired up the oven to bake bread. Abraham personally picked out and lassoed a fat calf. And because of all this, God made a promise to Abraham. Not even the most advanced fertility clinic today could have helped this couple conceive, yet God fulfilled his promise over the centuries that followed. He made this aged couple the grand-parents of billions.

The Bible makes one thing clear: God can work with the most unlikely of characters just as long as they believe God is who he says he is. Abraham was brave, except when he cowered. He was honest, except when he told half lies to save his own skin. He obeyed the Lord, except when he went off on his own to do things his own way. But Abraham always came back to the Lord.

Someone had to be the great father and mother of many nations whose line would lead to the Messiah, and God chose well with Abraham and Sarah.

God selected Abraham to occupy the place at the root of faith's tree. I think of the huge oak giving shade to Abraham and Sarah as the tree of hospitality. It's also called the Oak of Mamre. My century-old King James study Bible has three full-page plates depicting Abra-ham's Oak. An oak stands today at a site that is said to be the exact spot where the angels visited Abraham.

The First Planted Tree

Abraham arrived in Canaan, a stranger in a strange land. He owned no property, yet the Lord caused Abraham to become wealthy. Because of his bravery and wisdom, Abraham increasingly held sway over leaders in the area. Eventually, one of the local kings asked Abraham to enter into a peace treaty. Afterward, Abraham planted trees. This is the first record in the Bible that a human planted trees. Abraham paired his tree planting with an act of faith: "Abraham planted a grove in Beersheba, and called there on the name of the Lord, the everlasting God" (Genesis 21:33, kjv).

If you plant trees to celebrate important events—such as the birth of a child, the passing of a loved one, a friend's coming to faith, or the marriage of a family member— rest assured, you are in good company.

The Hebrew word for *grove* in this passage is understood to mean a group of tamarisk trees. Tamarisk trees grow well in arid climates, and they can even survive in areas of high salinity around the Dead Sea. The trees have a method of secreting salt and misting the area around themselves with water droplets. In so doing, they create a naturally cooled miniclimate. Abraham was a blessing; he planted trees to bless; and he called on the Lord.

If you plant trees to celebrate important events—such as the birth of a child, the passing of a loved one, a friend's coming to faith, or the marriage of a family member—rest assured, you are in good company.

Isaac's Wooden Cross

Abraham and Sarah doted on Isaac, their miracle baby. Years later, God asked Abraham to do something that seemed to come completely out of left field. God asked Abraham to make a human sacrifice of Isaac (Genesis 22:1–2).

Let's imagine what this father must have been thinking. He was instructed to take his beloved son and travel to a three-days-distant place. There he was told to climb a mountain and offer Isaac to the Lord. Nothing about this made sense. God was on record as opposing human sacrifice, so his command regarding Isaac went totally against Abraham's (and our) understanding of God. Yet Abraham complied. Why? Because Abraham believed that God could raise Isaac from the dead (Hebrews 11:17–19).

Abraham had seen God do the impossible again and again. So he gathered wood, a knife, two other men, and his son and began the journey. Abraham glanced at Isaac often. He had trouble swallowing. He tried not to think of Sarah. Meals passed silently. And on they traveled. Abraham looked at the sun and counted each passing hour. Time slowed.

Finally they reached the mountain, and Abraham and Isaac climbed. They reached the top of Calvary hill (for many believe this is the same place where another Son would be sacrificed two thousand years later). Abraham assured Isaac that God himself would provide a lamb for the sacrifice. Together Isaac and his father laid the wood for the pyre. Then Isaac, stronger than his father, held still while Abraham tied his son's hands behind his back.

A Ram Caught in the Branches

For three days in a row, I stared at Caravaggio's *Sacrifice of Isaac* painting in the Uffizi Gallery in Florence, Italy. It's horrifying. Death seems to be ready to pounce in a moment. And then death is swallowed up in victory. The son who has been dead to his father during a painful three-day trek is brought back to life. A thicket appears, and in its branches a ram is caught.

The scene of the testing of Abraham is a sketch for how the Son of God would save the world. It starts with an impossible birth of a promised son. Having committed no crime, the son is condemned to death. He carries wood on his shoulders to the top of a hill in what would become Jerusalem. Every preparation is carried out, and the son is bound and placed on the altar. In his father's mind the son has been dead for three days, ever since the funeral procession left Abraham's home.

Then the son comes back to life in a way no one could have foreseen. The son of promise is restored to his father. God's word is trustworthy. Now Abraham and Sarah can indeed become the ancestors of entire nations.

On every side Abraham's life was bounded by trees. He encountered a tree when he entered the Promised Land (Genesis 12:6), a tree where he met the Lord's angels (18:1, 4), and a tree where his son was to be sacrificed (22:13). Abraham planted a tree by an altar of the Lord (21:33). And he bought a plot of land that included a cave and all the surrounding trees when it came time to bury his bride, Sarah (23:17).

But why, you might ask, was the sacrificial ram caught in such a humble tree—a mere thicket?

God tends to do his most intimate business beside very small trees. If a tree is so small it appears to be a bush, look for God to be doing gigantic things—even the impossible.

When I began studying trees in the Bible, a pattern started to emerge. God tends to do his most intimate business beside very small trees. If a tree is so small it appears to be a bush, look for God to be doing gigantic things—even the impossible.

For now, let us rest in the shade for a moment. In one very real sense, we all can take shelter under Abraham's Oak. It can remind us that God provides and that we are meant to extend hospitality to strangers. We are meant to meet the Lord and call on his name. We are meant to give God our best, even a treasure as precious as our own children. And we are meant to plant trees. When we do so, we are acting like our great-grandfather Abraham and creating a more pleasant climate for generations yet to come.

5

The Wooden Ladder
to Heaven

A people without children would face a hopeless future;
a country without trees is almost as helpless.

—THEODORE ROOSEVELT

Before he died, Abraham made a provision for his son Isaac. He sent his chief servant back to Mesopotamia to find Isaac a wife. God led the servant to beautiful, kind, hardworking Rebekah (Genesis 24). Isaac and Rebekah had twin sons, Esau and Jacob. From the moment of their birth, the brothers clashed. When Jacob tricked Esau out of the blessing reserved for him as the firstborn, Rebekah and Isaac summoned Jacob and sent him packing. "Go to your uncle Laban's place and find yourself a wife. Your brother will cool off—eventually."

So with the shirt on his back and his walking staff in hand,

Jacob headed east toward his mother's childhood home. Throughout
the remainder of the Bible, the humble wooden walking stick was
standard issue for God's ministers and prophets. In biblical Hebrew
the word for "tree" and for "wood" is the same.

The humble wooden walking stick was standard issue for God's ministers and prophets. In biblical Hebrew the word for "tree" and for "wood" is the same.

Mile after mile, Jacob walked. By nightfall he was exhausted.
When he stopped, he threw a blanket over a rock and lay his head
down. As he drifted off to sleep, Jacob dreamed of heaven come to
earth.

JACOB'S LADDER—THE ALMOND TREES OF LUZ

We think of Palestine as a barren, arid region. But three thousand
years ago, the Holy Land was a place of forests. Two thousand years
ago Josephus described Israel's intact forests. A thousand years ago,
Richard the Lionheart fought an army that hid behind trees in this
area. I believe that on the night Jacob dreamed of a ladder, he saw
above him the outline of branches and leaves silhouetted against the
stars. Why? Because the place was called Luz, and *luz* is Hebrew for
"almond trees."

In his dream Jacob saw a ladder extending from the earth to
heaven. He saw angels ascending and descending on this ladder.

Jacob heard the Lord at the top of the ladder say, "Thy seed shall be as the dust of the earth, and thou shalt spread abroad to the west, and to the east, and to the north, and to the south: and in thee and in thy seed shall all the families of the earth be blessed"(28:14, KJV).

Jacob's vision may have inspired more works of art than any other dream in history. Everything from Chagall's painting of a simple wooden ladder to William Blake's illustration of an elegant spiral staircase has been used in an attempt to capture the essence of the scene. If you wish to walk around a three-dimensional depiction of Jacob's ladder, a trip to view the sculpture at Abilene Christian University should be high on your bucket list.

It's not a bad idea for those seeking God to approach the Bible as an artist would. Great artists see the truth in what happened long ago, and they translate those truths to our lives today. When they succeed, they don't transport us to the past so much as bring the past to the present.

The three depictions of Jacob's dream I mentioned are wildly different. Yet in conveying truth, each is as accurate as the others. They all tell of the divine moment when heaven and earth moved so close to each other that a wooden ladder could bridge the gulf.

When people approach the Bible as if they are anatomists dissecting a cadaver, they often end up with tendons, muscles, bones, and disconnected tissue but no idea of who God is. The Bible is not a wristwatch or other inanimate object whose parts can be isolated and deconstructed to gain insight into its purpose. Modern scholars smash atoms and peer into the depths of a cell's nucleus in a quest for understanding. But this method fails when it comes to God and the

Bible (2 Peter 1:20). One cannot kill a living being and then ask it questions. We may increase our understanding by closely examining the Bible, but we cannot dissect it to learn its thoughts. Faith is what breathes life into the Bible.

Let me illustrate. Suppose I do one of three things:

1. I tell you, "Anytime you need help, I want you to call me." I then hand you a cell phone.

2. I say, "If you ever get into trouble or run short of cash, use this." Then I hand you a credit card.

3. I hand you a set of keys to my house and car and say, "Keep these in case you need them."

Modern deconstructionists might argue that I have said three different things. They would dissect each of my offers into smaller and smaller units. Is it better for a person to get the phone, the credit card, or the keys? It depends, they would say, on how much battery life the cell phone has, what the credit card's limit is, and whether the house is a shack or a mansion and how much fuel is in the car's gas tank.

Jacob's ladder represents a connection between the ephemeral and eternal, between fallen and redeemed humanity.

Each question takes us further from the truth. The truth is that all three offers are the same. All say, "I'm here for you."

Likewise, the point of Jacob's dream is that God loves us. He is handing us a phone, his credit card, and the keys to paradise. He is bridging the distance between heaven and earth. This is the nature of God—he wants to draw us ever closer.

Jacob's ladder represents a connection between the ephemeral and eternal, between fallen and redeemed humanity. The ladder is a symbol of the Messiah. Later in the Bible, Christ will call a disciple from under a tree and explain Jacob's ladder (John 1:47–51).

JACOB'S STRIPPED BRANCHES

When Jacob awoke in the morning, he was overcome with awe and fear. God was present outdoors and under the trees, so he named the place the house of God (or *Bethel* in Hebrew; see Genesis 28:19).

Jacob poured oil on the rock where he'd laid his head and vowed to serve the Lord and to tithe if the Lord would someday bring him home. Then Jacob continued his journey. Weeks later at a well, he talked with men who tended sheep and learned that he'd arrived in the right place. As they spoke, a beautiful shepherdess arrived— Jacob's cousin Rachel. Jacob fell in love and agreed to work for seven years in order to marry Rachel. At the end of the agreed-upon period, his uncle Laban tricked him into first marrying Leah, Rachel's older sister. Laban promised that if Jacob would work for him another seven years, Jacob could marry Rachel.

At the end of fourteen years, Jacob had two wives, two concubines, a dozen children, and nothing in the bank. Laban, on the other hand, had gotten rich off Jacob's work. Jacob decided to head back home. But Laban knew his own wealth had grown because

God's hand was on Jacob. "Please stay," Laban pleaded. So Jacob agreed on one condition: from that point onward Laban would give Jacob all the oddly colored sheep and goats born to the flock.

To increase the number of oddly colored livestock, Jacob undertook a procedure using—you guessed it—trees. He stripped the bark off the branches of three different species of trees, and he put the flock in front of these branches at feeding and mating time (30:37–42).

STICKS AND MIRACLES

I tripped over this passage the first dozen times I read it. Even though I'd like for something to be going on with the branches Jacob set in front of the flock, his procedure is not scientific, nor is it presented as a miracle. What's going on?

As a medical resident I saw a case that sheds light on this matter. The patient, Mrs. Rose, was in her early eighties and lived independently. She arrived at the hospital with a high fever and shortness of breath. An x-ray confirmed a case of advanced pneumonia. She was so weak she couldn't walk. She needed intravenous antibiotics. There was a problem, though. No one could get an IV started because her veins were so fragile, and she didn't want a central line placed.

The attending physician thought we could treat her using a new oral antibiotic, so that's what we did. Her chances were not great. But within two days she started to turn around. She began to drink and then to eat.

Mrs. Rose was a delightful woman. She looked forward to the team making its rounds, and she was extravagant with her compliments. We went to see her before discharge. "I don't know what I would have done without you," she said, beaming. The attending physician grinned in return and pointed out that she would be dead if not for the antibiotics.

"Oh, I'm grateful for all you have done for me," she said. "I want to give you something you can pass on." She opened the drawer beside her bed and handed an envelope to the attending physician. It contained every pill she had been given while in the hospital. She hadn't taken a one.

Jacob's procedure with the sticks was like the antibiotics Mrs. Rose kept in the drawer. They had no bearing on the outcome. Sometimes patients recover for reasons no doctor can explain, and Mrs. Rose was one of them.

In Genesis 31:11–12, Jacob described a God-given vision in which the genetically recessive animals mated with one another to produce the offspring he needed. The massive increase in Jacob's odd-colored flock had nothing to do with Jacob or his bark-stripped branches. It came from God. Jacob might as well have put his sticks in a drawer.

God caused Jacob to prosper over the next seven years, and he acquired livestock galore. Laban began to resent Jacob for getting ahead financially. Eventually, God instructed Jacob to return to the Promised Land. Jacob and his wives, children, servants, sheep, donkeys, goats, and camels took their leave of Laban and headed home.

Here the text tells of one of the more unique roles of trees in the Bible. In Rachel and Jacob's flight, Rachel stole her father's idols. God told Jacob to head to Bethel and there to construct an altar. In turn, Jacob instructed the members of his household to cleanse and purify themselves. They did so, and Jacob buried the stolen idols under a terebinth tree (35:4).

We all have idols. We carry around useless images, habits, and memories we can't seem to separate ourselves from. I wonder if it might not help to write them on a piece of paper and, literally or figuratively, bury them under a tree.

THE TREE OF FORGIVENESS

Jacob had twelve sons, but Joseph was his favorite. Joseph's brothers sold him into slavery, but nonetheless he prospered and grew in his faith, eventually becoming the second-most-powerful leader in Egypt. Years later, when a seven-year famine plagued the land, Joseph forgave his brothers and provided them with food and fertile land. Without this act of kindness, Joseph's brothers and their families would have perished.

 Joseph is the Old Testament archetype of the person described in the first psalm: "a tree planted by streams of water, which yields its fruit in season and whose leaf does not wither."

Joseph repaid evil with goodness, murder with mercy, death with life. Indeed, many believe that Joseph's character is the closest representative of Christ we find in the Old Testament.

A few years ago, I told a friend that every major character in

Scripture is associated with a tree, branch, stick, or root. My friend really knows the Bible. I could see his mind whirling through the mental Rolodex. "What about Joseph?" he asked.

For a moment I thought I'd made a mistake. How could one of the most admirable characters in the Bible not have a tree associated with him? Then I remembered the blessing Jacob gave to his twelve sons shortly before his death: "Joseph is a fruitful bough, even a fruitful bough by a well; whose branches run over the wall" (49:22, KJV). Joseph *is* a tree! Joseph is the Old Testament archetype of the person described in the first psalm: "a tree planted by streams of water, which yields its fruit in season and whose leaf does not wither" (verse 3, NIV).

Judah's Boomerang Staff

Joseph's brother Judah represents the branch of Jacob's family that leads to the Messiah. In fact, the word *Jew* comes from Judah's name. At the end of Jacob's life when he blessed his sons, he predicted Judah's place in the messianic line. But Jacob also related a witticism about an incident in Judah's life, which had to do with trees.

Jacob said, "Judah is a lion's cub. . . . The scepter shall not depart from Judah, nor the ruler's staff from between his feet, until tribute comes to him; and to him shall be the obedience of the peoples" (Genesis 49:9–10). The staff of leadership could not pass from Judah, because this was God's plan. Not even Judah could subvert God's will.

But in chapter 38 we read that Judah attempted to cut off his place in the family tree of the Messiah. He had three sons: Er, Onan, and Shelah. Tamar married the first son, Er, who was so horrific that God killed him. Under the laws and customs of the day, Tamar then had a right to have sons by Er's next-oldest brother.

Judah gave Onan to Tamar so that she might conceive a son. But Onan shirked his duties, so God took him also. Judah suggested that Tamar live for a while as a widow with her father, and when Shelah was old enough, Judah would give him to Tamar. But years passed, and Judah ignored his promise.

Eventually Judah was widowed. He made plans to attend a sheepshearing event in a distant town. Tamar learned of his plans and decided to take matters into her own hands. She disguised herself as a prostitute and put a veil over her face. As she waited outside the town of the sheepshearing, Judah came along and asked how much it would cost to have sex with her. Seeing that he was empty handed, she asked for a goat. He promised to bring one later. When Tamar asked for collateral, he handed her his belt, ring, and walking staff.

Later, Judah sent a servant back to the town with a goat as payment to the prostitute, but she was nowhere to be found. Judah had little recourse but to allow the woman to keep his collateral.

Three months later, Judah got word that his daughter-in-law was pregnant. He decided to deal harshly with Tamar. When he asked that she be brought to him, she instead sent the belt, ring, and staff Judah had given her. She made it known that she was carrying the child of the man who owned the items given as collateral.

Judah was caught.

The son Tamar conceived with Judah passed the staff of leadership onward. In fact, the staff couldn't be removed from Judah's family even when he tried to give it away. His wooden staff bounced back like a boomerang from a woman named Tamar.

There are no coincidences in Scripture. God had a plan when he authored the Bible, and from beginning to end, he used trees to mark the trail.

Tamar means "palm tree." She appears in the family tree of Jesus and is named in the genealogy recorded in Matthew's gospel.

There are no coincidences in Scripture. God had a plan when he authored the Bible, and from beginning to end, he used trees to mark the trail.

6

The Bush Afire with God

> Earth's crammed with heaven,
> And every common bush afire with God:
> But only he who sees, takes off his shoes.
>
> —ELIZABETH BARRETT BROWNING,
> *Aurora Leigh*

When I worked as a physician, I rarely flew on planes. I really began traveling when I quit medicine and started talking to audiences about God. Left to my own desires, I'm a homebody and would rather stay put. But that wasn't in the plan, so I've learned to enjoy traveling.

My favorite thing about flying is landing in cities built near water. Add dramatic weather or lighting, and it's even better. And if the plane is swooping into a city at sunset, that's the best. Yet in the decade and a half I've been traveling by plane, I've noticed an ominous trend: people are losing sight of God's creation.

Recently, I flew over Lake Michigan on an approach to Chicago. The sun was setting, and red-gold cumulus clouds towered around us. Ships below plowed through the inland sea, leaving behind gleaming white wakes of drinking water.

Dazzling orange and red light poured through my window. It was as if the interior of the plane were somehow more real and tangible.

I looked to see if the people around me were enjoying the show. Not a single other passenger knew the sun was setting. Mine was the only open window shade on the plane.

Some passengers were asleep, but most were watching screens. Closing off the outside world in order to pay attention to screens is a recent phenomenon. It has emerged in the few years I've been flying.

Ramses the Great would have given a million slaves for a ride through the sky. For the same privilege Julius Caesar would have handed back Gaul and stopped short of the Rubicon.

Imagine if only one plane ride were left in the world. Imagine if tickets went on sale three years before the final flight. You could fill a jet at ten million dollars per seat or even a billion dollars a seat— and that would be before Christie's auctioned off tickets on the resale market.

Envision the commotion if a window seat became available a month before the last-ever flight. *The Times* would interview and publish in-depth profiles of the passengers. A television series would follow their progress.

One of the lovely things about the Bible is that God occasionally rewards the reader with glimpses over the horizon. The Bible is written not only in many literary forms but also from various points of view. Some are out of this world. God—being omnipotent—gazes on the universe from many vantage points.

The bejeweled line that stretches around the earth at the junction of light and dark, described in Job 26:10, is something only our generation can fully appreciate. But is it any less a miracle to walk on the ground of the only living planet known to exist in the universe? What would we give to walk on grass, swim in a lake, jump in maple leaves, catch fireflies, smell flowers, or taste snow on a mitten if we had been raised under a dome on Mars?

People grow bored by what they have ready access to, even if it is a miracle. No wonder God doesn't show up at our bidding.

The Burning Bush

The airplane interior alight with the setting sun is akin to one of the most famous stories in the Bible: the one with Moses standing in front of a burning bush.

Four centuries had passed since Jacob and his family settled in Egypt, and the number of their adult male descendants had grown from seventy to six hundred thousand. In the intervening years the Hebrew people had become slaves under a cruel pharaoh. Moses, the son of Hebrew parents, killed an Egyptian slave master and ran away to Midian. Forty years later, God reached out to the exiled Moses using an unusual sign. Moses was out tending the flock on the western slope of Mount Horeb when he saw a peculiar sight.

The angel of the LORD appeared to him in a flame of fire out of the midst of a bush. He looked, and behold, the bush was burning, yet it was not consumed. And Moses said, "I will turn aside to see this great sight, why the bush is not burned." When the LORD saw that he turned aside to see, God called to him out of the bush, "Moses, Moses!" And he said, "Here I am." (Exodus 3:2–4)

Why did God use a humble bush? Why didn't God call to Moses from a towering tree? The picture of God speaking from a lowly bush reminds me of a father stooping down to talk to his small children. This imagery of God using small trees or lowly bushes to speak to his people repeats itself in Scripture.

> One of the dangers of not pausing to appreciate the glories of creation—including the trees in God's world and God's Word—is that we limit our ability to appreciate what God is up to.

What I find intriguing, however, is the comment Moses made to himself: "I will turn aside to see this great sight." The sight is a bush burning, not a forest fire. Yet Moses saw the sight and turned aside. What if he had been staring at his cell phone? One of the dangers of not pausing to appreciate the glories of creation—including the trees in God's world and God's Word—is that we limit our ability to appreciate what God is up to.

Also, note that God did not speak to Moses until Moses noticed the burning bush. If we want to hear from God, we need to pay attention to miracles God places in front of us—even if it means turning off the television.

CALLING DISCIPLES FROM TREES

God often uses trees when calling his people. In Scripture God called to Gideon (Judges 6:11), Nathanael (John 1:48), and Zacchaeus (Luke 19:1–6) with, through, and in trees.

Joan of Arc heard God speak to her when she was in her father's garden. Augustine spoke of hearing the voice of a child while sitting under a fig tree. Martin Luther met God when Luther sought shelter under a tree during a violent thunderstorm. And God still uses trees when he calls his disciples. Over the past decade and a half, I've met at least a dozen people who have received their calling into ministry while sitting near, under, or in a tree.

God called Moses from a bush. This bush, though fragile, passed through the fire alive, just as all true believers in God shall pass unscathed through the fires of death into eternal life.

MOSES'S WALKING STICK
AND THE HYSSOP BRANCHES

When God first called Moses to free the Hebrew people, Moses didn't believe Pharaoh would listen to him. So God called attention to Moses's wooden walking stick, a staff made from a tree. The prophet's walking stick is referred to as the "rod of God." Equipped with the rod of God, Moses and his older brother, Aaron, went back to Egypt to do battle against Pharaoh.

In addition to the walking stick, ten plagues from God were needed to convince Pharaoh to let Moses and his people go. These plagues represent more than a battle between Moses and Pharaoh. Each is a matchup between God and the gods of Egypt: "On all the gods of Egypt I will execute judgments: I am the LORD" (Exodus 12:12). God's plague of darkness blotted out the light of Ra, the Egyptian sun god. The frogs were a defeat of Heqet, the frog goddess. The plague of diseased cattle defeated the Apis bull and the goddess Hathor, and so on. The magicians of Egypt mimicked the first two plagues Moses summoned, leaving Pharaoh unimpressed by the God of the Hebrews. But when the Lord sent tiny gnats to cover man and beast, Pharaoh's magicians declared, "This is the finger of God" (8:19). The might of Egypt was laid low by gnats.

When Pharaoh reneged yet again on his promise to let the slaves leave Egypt, God gave instructions for the first Passover. Each Hebrew household was to kill a lamb, to be eaten later during the evening meal. The Hebrews were to dip hyssop branches in the lamb's blood and use the green hyssop leaves, afire with the blood of the lamb, to seal the house's wooden door and lock out the angel of death.

This combination of lamb's blood and wood spelled liberation for the people who had been held in bondage. On Passover night the Hebrew people ate the body of the lamb in solemn and expectant stillness as the angel of death visited the firstborn of Egypt.

What a terrible night it was. By morning hundreds of thousands of firstborn Egyptians lay dead, including Pharaoh's son. The Egyptians wanted nothing more to do with the Hebrew people. The twelve tribes of Israel lined up carrying the sarcophagus that held Joseph's body. Then the six hundred thousand men along with women, children, and cattle made a procession out of Egypt. The blood of a sacrificed lamb painted on a wooden doorpost saved the Hebrew people from death.

THE ROD OF GOD

In Exodus 14, the Hebrew people approached the edge of the Red Sea with Pharaoh and his armored chariots in hot pursuit. The unarmed masses were in a panic. Moses lifted his staff above the sea, and the waters parted. The tribes of Israel walked across the Red Sea on dry ground.

After the freed Hebrews crossed over, Moses stretched out his hand, and the waters that were piled up in a wall came crashing down on the pursuing Egyptian army. How the Egyptian people must have gasped when they learned of this. Not only was their god-king dead, but even more unthinkable, his body was lost.

When we consider the decades that a pharaoh spent preparing to journey to the afterworld, we can begin to understand what a devastating defeat this was. In ancient Egypt no corpse meant no body to mummify and no mummy to make it to the afterlife. Ironically, however, the Hebrew people carried Joseph's four-century-old embalmed body across the dry seafloor to be laid to rest in the Promised Land.

Sweet Wood

The Hebrews journeyed in the wilderness. For three days they found no water, and the people grumbled to Moses. When they finally came to a place with water, the water was bitter and undrinkable. So the Lord instructed Moses to cast a log into the water, "and the water became sweet" (15:25). This log is a foreshadowing of the cross. The cross is the tree that makes the bitter waters of life sweet.

The cross is the tree that makes the bitter waters of life sweet.

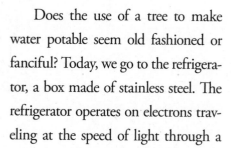

Does the use of a tree to make water potable seem old fashioned or fanciful? Today, we go to the refrigerator, a box made of stainless steel. The refrigerator operates on electrons traveling at the speed of light through a web of power lines connected to a plant that splits atoms. We press a glass to a lever in the door of the refrigerator, and a light-emitting diode illuminates a stream of water pouring into our glass. The water is cooled by the compression and expansion of gases unknown to the ancient world. The scene and the technology would have seemed alien to Moses. But oddly, in the back of the refrigerator is a filter for the water, and inside the filter of this space-age technology is wood. Trees in the form of charcoal are still making water sweet. God chose metaphors that have lasted into the age of nuclear-powered appliances.

THE ORIGINAL PALM SPRINGS

The people traveled onward and came to Elim, a Hebrew word for "palms." At this Palm Springs were "twelve springs of water and seventy palm trees" (15:27). Seventy is a significant number; it represents the number of members in Joseph's family who originally came to Egypt. Twelve is the number of tribes traveling with Moses. The palm tree is henceforth associated with Judah and the Hebrew nation. When Vespasian conquered Judaea in AD 70, he minted a coin showing Judaea as a woman sitting under a date palm and weeping.

As the Hebrews continued traveling, they went without water for another three days. A riot was brewing, and the people wanted to stone Moses. So Moses cried to the Lord, and God told him, "Pass on before the people, taking with you some of the elders of Israel, and take in your hand the staff with which you struck the Nile, and go. Behold, I will stand before you there on the rock at Horeb, and you shall strike the rock, and water shall come out of it, and the people will drink" (17:5–6). Moses struck the rock once, and water gushed out.

The descendants of Esau—the Amalekites—attacked Moses and his people. To defeat the attacking forces, Moses gave Joshua command of an army. During the battle Moses stood on a hill, staff (tree branch) in hand, praying (verses 8–13).

At the point in Exodus where Moses strikes the rock with a stick, we are less than two books into the Bible. Already a pattern of

interactions between trees, God, and humanity is emerging. This
pattern is as clear and repetitive as the patterns in a toddler's board
book, yet still we miss it. The first humans were put in the garden
with trees and told to dress and keep the trees; instead, they ate from
the wrong tree, so they weren't allowed to eat from the good one.
They were banished from the garden of trees, and much later a man
named Noah built an ark using wood from trees. A dove landed on
the ark, near the end of the flood, carrying a leaf from a tree in its
mouth. Much later, Abraham met angels under a tree, and then
Abraham's son Isaac was rescued by a ram caught in a tree.

Then one of Abraham's grandsons (Judah) tried to give away a
tree, and another of his grandsons (Joseph) was called a tree. As we
just saw, Moses met God at a burning tree and went to Pharaoh with
a walking stick made from a tree branch. Moses used the stick to part
the sea, make the water in the wilderness sweet, bring water out of a
rock, and ensure victory for Joshua's army. As we will see in the coming chapters, the tree-God-gospel connection only grows as we follow the Hebrew nation through the wilderness and beyond.

WHICH HAS MORE TREES:
HEAVEN OR HELL?

Here is a good time to pause and reflect on humanity's larger stewardship mandate, the Genesis 2:15 command for people to care for
God's creation. Like the pattern of trees we've been tracing, the larger
creation-care mandate runs from Genesis to Revelation. "The earth

is the LORD's and the fullness thereof," Psalm 24:1 thunders, signing God's name to the earth's title and deed.

The earth and everything on it belong to God, not us. We are given dominion as God's appointed stewards, but that dominion implies tremendous responsibility.

Let's suppose a friend lent you his new car. Would you return it smelling like stale cigarettes, the back seat littered with bottles, and the car doors dented? I think not,

> We don't need more wonders; we need a greater sense of wonderment.

at least if you had any respect for your friend. Rather, you would return the car with a full tank of gas and a wax job.

Likewise, we should pass along the earth, from one generation to the next, in as good or better shape than we received it. We are but sojourners; God is the earth's rightful and permanent owner.

And God is in the life business. Therefore, we, the crown jewel of God's creation, are called to be wise stewards of everything that supports life.

Trees support life at multiple levels: They purify the air and are responsible for water and rain being able to travel more than three hundred miles inland. Trees are home to one-half of all the creatures that live on land. They give us food and shade. They are one of the first things children learn to draw. And they give us chocolate! Trees sweeten our lives on so many levels.

As God's appointed stewards, we are also told to make the earth a little more like heaven (Matthew 6:10). We should therefore ask ourselves, "Which brings heaven closer—planting or destroying trees?" Put another way, "Which has more trees—heaven or hell?" (Hint: trees need water.)

Planting and protecting trees are just a couple of ways we can fulfill our Genesis 2:15 mandate to be good stewards.

THE TREES GET THEIR DAY IN COURT

Someday Jesus will return to judge the earth. The prudent fear this day (Amos 5:18). Each of us knows that we are guilty of many misdeeds. Indeed, the Bible describes people hiding under rocks and in caves in fear of God's wrath on Judgment Day (Isaiah 2:19; Revelation 6:16).

Trees, however, do the opposite. They shout for joy. They finally get their day in court, and for once an honest judge is on the bench. They know how the ruling will go (1 Chronicles 16:33; Psalm 96:11–13). This judge has not been bribed or buttered up, and his judgment has not been clouded. When the gavel comes down, God rules in favor of the trees. The trees win.

As if to underscore this ruling, Revelation 11:18 says, "The nations raged, but your wrath came, and the time for the dead to be judged, and for rewarding your servants, the prophets and saints, and those who fear your name, both small and great, and for destroying the destroyers of the earth." On Judgment Day God will destroy the destroyers of the earth. Take my advice: you may not be for trees, but don't go on record as being against them. The destroyers of trees will have to face God's wrath on Judgment Day.

WONDER AND WONDERMENT

"But what if I don't care about trees?" you may ask. God's ways are not our ways. Many aspects of God's character, including his likes and dislikes, go against the natural grain of humanity. Indeed, I've had to work hard to change things in my life and character that don't come naturally to me. Sometimes we have to fake it till we make it when it comes to doing things God's way.

Don't care for trees? My advice is to start small. Plant a seed or a seedling. Water it. Care for it. You'll be surprised by what will happen. You'll begin to see the world more like God does from his throne in heaven.

We can't be good stewards of creation unless we open our eyes, our minds, and sometimes our window shades to see things from God's perspective. We don't need more wonders; we need a greater sense of wonderment.

7

The Gardener of Israel

Let the trees of the forest sing for joy before the LORD,
for he is coming to judge the earth.

—1 CHRONICLES 16:33, NLT

Long before sustainable agriculture became popular, God set up guidelines for the good of the land and people. For example, a newly planted tree was not to be harvested for the first three years (Leviticus 19:23). This is still sound agricultural advice today.

Further, fruit trees were not to be beaten twice (Deuteronomy 24:20)—meaning when the Hebrew people were harvesting almonds, olives, and dates, they were to leave some fruit and nuts behind to be gleaned by birds and the poor. Moreover, every seven years, trees were not to be harvested at all (Leviticus 25:3–4).

Clearly, the Bible is concerned with a greater good than short-term profit—agricultural or otherwise. Adopting a more godlike perspective is best for trees and for humanity. And a godlike perspective takes a longer view.

THE FOUNDING FATHER
OF SUSTAINABLE AGRICULTURE

Here's another relevant mandate: the Hebrew people were never to cut down a fruit tree, even in the direst circumstances, such as in a time of war: "Are the trees your enemies, that you should attack them?" (Deuteronomy 20:19, NLT). Most experts agree that deforested places such as Haiti and sub-Saharan Africa won't be lifted out of poverty until the land is reforested and the existing trees are protected.

The Bible's thousands-year-old agricultural principles still hold true. People who plant trees are not going into business for themselves; they are going into business with God. How different this is from the approach some take today that removes God, wildlife, and the next generation's well-being from the equation.

Another biblical law prohibited harvesting to the edge of a field (Leviticus 23:22). The farms where I grew up generally ranged from sixty to three hundred acres. These farms were further subdivided into fields, pastures, barnyard, farmhouse, tenement lots, and woodlots ranging in size from several acres to thirty acres each. Fence lines and hedgerows ranging in width from a few feet to a dozen feet separated the fields. When added together, these untilled areas accounted for many acres on a large farm. The land that bordered the fields was the equivalent of the protected land at the edge of the field described in the Bible. To a large extent this landscape still predominates in portions of Europe and farms in the eastern United States.

In part, the American Dust Bowl of the 1930s resulted from removing the fence lines and hedgerows from farms as small landholdings were combined to form larger and larger estates. Without the natural barriers on the edges of the tilled fields, there was nothing to stop erosion and retain runoff water. During the Dust Bowl, the federal government planted nearly a quarter of a billion trees to combat the damage done to the landscape by the wholesale removal of fence breaks and the practice of excessive plowing.

Unless you've spent significant time walking along these perimeters, you might have no idea of the wonder and life that exist within them. These areas are home to the sparrow and the woodchuck. This is where indigo buntings build their nests. This is where rabbits flee when the hay is cut. These areas account for much of the beauty on a farm.

Even a field in the fallow season is alive with purpose. In the fall migrating flocks land in the fields to rest and glean corn missed by the combine. A bit of snow on a harvested field is a masterpiece. No color combination is as subtle as flaxen-gold cornstalks against a background of snow with the sun setting. Outline such a field with trees and you're working on perfection.

God is close at hand in the fields and woods. Unfortunately, when I was a kid, no one told me so. The theological move to disconnect God from the natural world was well underway by the time I was born. The succession of pastors who preached in the little church near our house forgot to mention that God made special provisions in his laws for the peach, pear, and apple trees planted on the farms around us (Deuteronomy 20:19).

WORSHIPPING THE CREATION
RATHER THAN THE CREATOR

People will worship almost anything: comic book characters, food, drugs, cars—even animals. When Moses came down the mountain carrying God's commandments, he found a nation worshipping a calf made of gold.

Moses "took the calf they had made and burned it. Then he ground it into powder, threw it into the water, and forced the people to drink it" (Exodus 32:20, NLT). He was furious, in essence saying, "If you want your idol back, you're going to have to get it out of your own manure. That's what I think of your glittering cow god."

I've heard a concern voiced about trees. It goes something like this: "If Christians care for God's creation, aren't we on the slippery slope to worshipping trees?" Of course, people might worship trees. People will worship pretty much anything, and trees are no exception.

However, slippery-slope arguments made by people with hidden agendas can be one of the devil's best tactics to keep us from right action. The devil gains almost as much by paralyzing us as convincing us to act in the wrong way. Having a proper regard for trees is no more the slippery slope to idolatry than giving a bowl of rice to a starving child is a slippery slope to gluttony.

A more productive question might be to ask why people would worship anything other than God. Here's the answer: we were made to worship. We have no choice in the matter. The only choice we have is what we are going to worship.

> **The human body runs on oxygen and the energy stored in carbon bonds. That's how our bodies work. The human soul was built to run on communion with God. That's how our souls work.**

The human body runs on oxygen and the energy stored in carbon bonds. That's how our bodies work. The human soul was built to run on communion with God. That's how our souls work.

The soul has no more ability to get out of this arrangement than the human body does to give up breathing oxygen. Yes, it would be easier if we ran on nitrogen. The atmosphere contains three times as much of it, and it's safer to handle than oxygen. But oxygen is what makes our metabolism run.

Similarly, the human soul was designed to be in a relationship with something greater than itself. This *something* is God. Our ability to choose the object of our soul's affection defines us as humans just as it separates us from all other creatures on the earth. Our souls were meant to run on God—but trees, humans, and even pets have all been used as substitutes (2 Kings 17:33).

So yes, people can and have worshipped trees. Yet I think a far more likely scenario is to worship God *as well as* other idols. What do I mean by that? For every tree worshipper I've encountered in the last decade, I've met hundreds more polytheists. They go to church on Sundays unless they have a more important god to worship. Then they worship a golden calf, bull, the Eagles, Lions, Tigers, Bears, Ravens, Rams, and other gods that anyone in the ancient pagan world would have easily recognized. Ask any pastor what will empty out a church on Sundays, and the answer will not be tree worshipping. It will be the modern equivalent of Baal, which is now spelled *Ball*.

MADE IN THE SHADE

When we last saw Moses, he had led the Hebrew nation to the door of the Promised Land. His successor was Joshua, who led the people across the Jordan River. At the end of Joshua's life, he warned the Hebrew nation never to serve other gods. They were to eschew the pagan religion of the surrounding Canaanites. "Never make a god, idol, or golden calf. Never bow down to one or serve it," Joshua told them. Joshua placed a stone under a tree to remind the Hebrew nation not to go astray (Joshua 24:26).

Joshua was as far from being a tree worshipper as you can find. He was the one who famously said, "As for me and my house, we will serve the LORD" (verse 15). Yet Joshua used a tree to mark the spot where he'd warned the people about idolatry.

Following Joshua's death, a period began in which judges governed Israel. During one period Deborah was the judge of the nation. No kings ruled Israel at this time, so the judge was the commander in chief, the Senate, and the Supreme Court all put together. God's Torah was the Constitution and the Bill of Rights.

Deborah held court under palm trees. She and her military commander, Barak, won a great battle against the invading general, Sisera. Shortly after their victory, Deborah and Barak went into the studio and recorded their hit duet. You can read the lyrics in the book of Judges (5:2–31).

When the song ends, the Bible records a striking line: "And the land had rest for forty years" (verse 31). *The land rested for forty years!* If I had a time machine and could beam back to the ancient world, this forty-year period would be a time and place I'd love to visit. The Promised Land was at peace, with every man and woman eating the fruit of their own vines and orchards and each generation planting for the next. The hearts of the parents were turned toward their children, and the hearts of the children were turned to their parents. Evenings were spent outdoors watching the sunset, with children hunting glowworms. It was a time when you didn't worry about the kids because everyone was watching out for them.

Such periods of peace are rare. And what ended the peace wasn't an invading army, the plague, or a drought. What ended the peace was the fickle heart of the people and their forgetfulness about God's jealousy.

NOT ALL RELIGIONS LEAD TO THE SAME PLACE

After Deborah ended her term as judge, the people did what was evil in the sight of the Lord. They began to worship the Canaanite god Baal and Baal's consort, Asherah. And Hebrew society began to unravel.

Many people today believe that one religion is much like another. But the historical record is at odds with this philosophy. We can look to the Bible to see what happened when people turned from God to Baal.

In general, gods in the ancient world were specialists. One might control the sea (Poseidon) or a specific place such as the hearth (Hestia). Baal was the god of the wind and clouds, while Asherah was the goddess of fertility. The Bible uses the term *Asherah pole* to denote a totem pole set up at an Asherah worship site. The site might also include live trees—a so-called sacred grove.

If you look up Baal and Asherah on the internet or in reference books, be prepared for confusion. The gods of the thirteenth century BC were a slippery lot. Just as Dionysus became Bacchus and Zeus became Jupiter or Jove as Romans renamed Greek gods, so, too, the gods of the Egyptians, the Canaanites, and surrounding cultures exchanged traits, names, and relationships as other cultures modified and adopted them. Much of what we know about them is little more than speculation. No example of an Asherah pole has ever been found, but mounds of small charred bones have been exhumed by the spades of archaeologists. Worship of Baal and Asherah definitely was linked to the sacrifice of children.

The prophet Jeremiah described the Lord's revulsion at the practice of killing children: "They have filled this place with the blood of innocents, and have built the high places of Baal to burn their sons in the fire as burnt offerings to Baal, which I did not command or decree, nor did it come into my mind" (Jeremiah 19:4–5).

If Baal was the god of the clouds and a sacrifice would entice him to send rain, and if a nation's fertility was failing because of the drought, might not a sacrifice to both the god of the sky and the goddess of fertility be twice as effective? To those who think that all spiritual paths lead to the same place, a study of child sacrifice and the religions that gave rise to it is a sobering road map.

As a doctor I made a lot of children cry. I had to insert IVs, tap spines, and set bones. Of course the parents, nurses, and I were all trying our very best to help each child. Yet imagine if the child's best interests were not our motivation. Imagine if the child were going to be mutilated and burned alive.

In ancient times child sacrifice was integral to appeasing the god Baal, especially in times of calamity. As a sacrificial ceremony progressed, the child's screams would grow more and more shrill. His or her screams could become bloodcurdling as priests of Baal cut off the child's ears or private parts.

Archaeological digs attest to such atrocities. And tragically, human sacrifice is still practiced today. Uganda even has an Anti-Human Sacrifice and Trafficking Task Force. Recently, one Ugandan mother described how her eight-year-old son's body was found in a swamp, his teeth, ears, and genitals missing. He had been sacrificed by a witch doctor—perhaps to encourage the gods to send rain.[2] God's injunction against worshipping idols has real-world consequences.

GIDEON CALLED FROM
UNDERNEATH A TREE

Because the Hebrew people started worshipping Baal, the Lord withdrew his protection from Israel. Then Midianites oppressed the people for seven years, which put the Israelites in a state of slow starvation. At harvest time, the Midianites came and stole the crops.

Under these conditions we encounter a man who was pitted against tree worshipping, and God called him from—of all things—a tree. Gideon's story began in the hill country inhabited by the tribe of Manasseh in ancient Israel. In an effort to hide his activities from the Midianite invaders, Gideon furtively threshed his grain in a winepress under the shade of a tree.

Gideon looked up and saw a beautiful sight: an angel of the Lord, who said, "The LORD is with you, O mighty man of valor" (Judges 6:12). The angel spoke while sitting on one of the giant roots at the base of an ancient tree. In his hand the angel held a wooden walking staff. The angel told Gideon to go and save Israel from the Midianites.

When Gideon asked how he could do this—considering he came from the weakest family in his tribe and was the youngest of his brothers—the angel of the Lord simply replied, "I will be with you" (verse 16).

That night the Lord gave Gideon instructions to cut down the Asherah poles of his father and to lay waste his father's altar to Baal. Under the cover of darkness, Gideon carried out God's instructions. The next morning the neighbors found the smoldering remains of the pagan altar. When the townsfolk discovered it was Gideon's doing, they sought to stone him.

But Gideon's father stood up for his son: "If Baal really is a god, he can defend himself when someone breaks down his altar" (verse 31, NIV). This marked a turning point in Gideon's relationship with God and his people. The Spirit of the Lord came over Gideon, and he blew a ram's horn. Men from many tribes came running with their weapons, prepared to go to battle.

FLEECE UNDER A TREE

Gideon sought assurance from God before he went into battle: "If I'm to defeat the Midianites, please give me a sign, Lord. I'll put a lamb's fleece out at night under the tree, and if in the morning it is wet and the ground around it is dry, I'll know that you want me to attack" (see verses 36–37).

Gideon put a fleece on the threshing floor by the tree. In the morning the ground was dry and the fleece was soaked.

Still unsure, he prayed for the Lord's indulgence and reversed the conditions: "If I put a fleece out and it stays dry and the ground is soaked, I'll know that you are really with me" (see verse 39). The following morning the fleece was dry and the ground was soaked.

PURAH, THE TREE BRANCH

God sent Gideon into the Midianite camp by cover of night with his servant, Purah. The two sneaked toward the enemy and learned that a great fear had come over the Midianites and the person they feared was Gideon.

Gideon divided his three hundred men into groups of one hundred. Then at his signal they blew trumpets and suddenly lit lamps all around the enemy's camp. A panic ensued, and in the dark the enemy fell upon one another (7:9–23).

There's a curious detail about the servant whom God told Gideon to take along. Purah's name means "bough of a tree"—or "tree branch."

WHERE THERE ARE TREES, THERE IS LIFE

Long before humans knew that trees were keeping the air on, God used them as a symbol of life. Trees give us food, water, shelter, and clothing. They regulate the climate locally and worldwide. They give us shade, and they give us beauty. Until the last two centuries, they were the primary way to heat a home in winter. Without trees life on the earth would be impossible.

Without trees life on the earth would be impossible.

And this is why, even in a world that sacrificed children to Asherah and other idols, God called Gideon from under a tree.

This is why God has used a group of people named after Gideon to hurl his story across thousands of years and to put a Bible in nearly every hotel room and hospital across this land.

Thank you, Gideon. I owe you.

8

The Tree of Hope

> At least there is hope for a tree:
>> If it is cut down, it will sprout again,
>> and its new shoots will not fail.
>
> —Job 14:7, NIV

No one is happy when a tree is blown down. We shake our heads and feel sadness when we see a familiar old tree upended. The same is not true for humans. Some dark part of humanity actually seems to enjoy the downfall of other people. This appetite is most satisfied if the person in question falls from a great height.

The Bible chronicles the fall of a person so stellar that we might wonder if such a noble character will ever appear again. He had wealth, power, friends, family, and a loving wife. He lived in a beautiful neighborhood. He was known as a *mensch*—the Yiddish term for someone who is admired and emulated. He didn't cheat on his taxes. He helped the poor get work. He built a wing on the children's hospital and even paid for the parking garage. Job was a man who kept his word.

And as you might have guessed, the story of someone this noble is bound to include a tree.

Job's Homeland Was a Wooded Place

Job lived in the land of Uz. *Uz* is a non-Hebrew Semitic word that means "wooded place." This is the perfect location for the story of Job since we find a tree at the heart of the tale. (Maybe you live in The Woodlands, Forest Hills, Maple Grove, Pineville, or perhaps even Hollywood.)

It is a safe guess that Job lived in a city with well-tended shade trees. In the days before air-conditioning—meaning all but the last few seconds on the time line of human history—shade trees made it possible for people to live comfortably in warm climates. The Bible tells us that Job was blameless and upright, a man who feared God and turned away from evil. His children enjoyed one another's company and respected their father.

After introducing Job's family, the book of Job switches to a scene taking place in heaven. Enter Satan, the only figure in the Bible who introduced himself to God as busy. The scene opens with Satan arriving late to a meeting.

"Where have you come from?" God asked.

"I've been zipping up and down and going back and forth on the earth," said the devil. "I've been working like the . . . well, myself," the devil declared.

The conversation between God and Satan then turned to Job. Job was the noblest man on the earth. However, Satan disparaged Job's virtue. "If you didn't watch over him," the devil taunted, "Job would curse you just like everyone else."

This was not only an insult to Job; it was also meant to malign the Lord. In his insult Satan accused Job of opportunistic motives— caring about God only for what he could get out of the relationship. The devil also implied that God is unlovable.

God pointed out that Satan was wrong, yet the Lord agreed to withdraw his protection from Job and his family (see Job 1:1–12).

HOPE UPROOTED

Tragedy quickly descended on the house of Job. His children and servants were killed, and his possessions were taken. Still, Job did not curse God. Instead, he praised the Lord: "The LORD gave, and the LORD has taken away; blessed be the name of the LORD" (verse 21).

The devil then took away Job's health. Job was covered from head to toe with sores. The sores oozed and itched. Picture the worst case of poison sumac/hives/measles you've ever seen, and then multiply it by one hundred. Job used the sharp edge of a pottery shard to scrape his lesions. When his wife saw him, she said, "Do you still hold fast your integrity? Curse God and die" (2:9).

Three of Job's friends then traveled to be with him. Job looked so ghastly that at first the trio didn't recognize him. For a week the men sat in silence on a heap of trash. All was well until the three friends opened their mouths. The squabble that followed was akin to a married couple going over and over the same ground without moving forward. The friends asserted that Job had hidden sin and that he brought miseries upon himself. They were wrong, but since when has being wrong stopped people from arguing? The friends merely doubled and tripled down on their assertions.

At his lowest point Job cried out, "He breaks me down on every side, and I am gone, and my hope has he pulled up like a tree" (19:10). Yet no matter how despondent he became, Job never gave up on his belief that God is good. Oh, Job would have liked a few words with his Maker, but he still held fast to his faith. Centuries later, James cited Job as one of the most patient and enduring men in all of history (James 5:11).

Hope Sprouts Again

Satan heaped tragedy upon tragedy on Job. Job bent, but his faith did not break. At one point he wished that he were a tree: "For there is hope for a tree, if it be cut down, that it will sprout again, and that its shoots will not cease. Though its root grow old in the earth, and its stump die in the soil, yet at the scent of water it will bud and put out branches like a young plant" (14:7–9).

In this respect, humans and trees are as different as night is from day. You can't take a finger, put it in the ground, and grow a person. But oddly, you can take a cutting from a tree and grow a new one. Here on the pages of the book of Job, the protagonist gives voice to a phenomenon that tree scientists are just beginning to understand.

Growing up in farming country, I helped put in fences. I remember setting black locust posts, and a year later the posts sported new branches and leaves. (In times gone by, posts were planted close enough that branches could be woven together to make an impenetrable hedge—a practice known as pleaching.)

Trees are always trying to come back to life. Cut one down, and the story isn't necessarily over. A German forester recently recounted finding buried wood from a stump, the remnant of a tree cut down centuries before. The wood still had living chlorophyll present. It was getting the chlorophyll through webs of interconnecting fungal growths terminating at living trees.[3]

It seems that trees will even share sap and chlorophyll with fallen neighbors. Whether through seed, scion, stump, or fence post, trees tenaciously cling to life. Moreover, trees challenge the human model of what is alive and what is dead. As Job exclaimed, there is hope for a tree *even* if it is cut down.

> Trees are always trying to come back to life. Cut one down, and the story isn't necessarily over.

Imagine losing your family, love, public standing, finances, and health, all in one fell swoop. And then, even though Job was the most honest man on the earth, his three closest friends accused him of being a liar. Still, Job did not curse God. For most people a stubbed toe, a lost phone, or a spilled cup of coffee is enough to occasion a reflexive curse, but not for Job.

In the midst of his misery, Job made one of the most beautiful assertions in all of Scripture. He said he knew beyond a doubt that like a tree, he would live again, even if he were cut down. "For I know that my Redeemer lives, and at the last he will stand upon the earth. And after my skin has been thus destroyed, yet in my flesh I shall see God" (19:25–26).

A man named Elihu had been listening to the debate and joined the discussion. Elihu was younger than the trio who had been prosecuting Job. Elihu spent less time harassing Job and more time espousing God's qualities. As he talked, he alluded to a storm in the distance. If you have ever sat in silence in a deep wood and heard a storm coming, you may know the wonder of hearing the wind approaching in the trees. When the storm arrived, God was in the midst of the whirlwind.

SCIENCE CURRICULUM
BEFORE SCIENTIFIC DISCOVERIES

What followed is the longest extended monologue from God's lips to our ears in Scripture. God was on the scene, in the house, and holding court. "Dress for action like a man; I will question you," God thundered (38:3), but it was almost as if God winked at Job and whispered, "I'll take it from here."

"Where were you when I laid the foundation of the earth?" God famously asked (verse 4).

And then the Creator proceeded to lay out the curriculum for colleges and universities for the next several thousand years. "Do you know about oceanography? Have you studied plant physiology or the reproductive cycles of mammals? Have you invented meteorology yet? If maternal instincts are needed for survival, why do some species have them and others do not? Do you know why so few animals can be domesticated? For goodness' sake, you won't establish wilderness parks for thousands of years, yet I see the value of them now."

God asked if Job and his friends could bind the 250 stars in the Pleiades and move them in the same direction as a flock. Conversely, did the four men know that the three star formations in Orion's belt are unbound and have no gravitational relationship to one another? Could they bring forth Arcturus and the fifty-two stars in the Arcturus stream ("the Bear with its children") at great speed (chapters 38–41)?

It almost seems as if God were daring us to invent the telescope and have a look-see for ourselves. In all these questions God was suggesting an order, timing, and laws that neither Job nor humanity were yet aware of, much less understood. We read these statements and others like them in the Bible through the fog of repetition and familiarity. As a result, we miss the wonder of God's questions. How could any author other than the Creator of the universe know to ask them?

Scholars believe that Job is one of the oldest books of the Bible, a story written thousands of years ago, yet there are no mistakes— nothing that contradicts current scientific discoveries.

God was not asking Job and his friends about all the bunny trails that academia has traveled down over the last three thousand years. For example, the book of Job does not mention alchemy, transmutation of metals, or phrenology. The encyclopedias of Aristotle, Cato, Varro, and Pliny, however, failed to avoid these pitfalls. The Bible avoided these mistakes because its author understands every nook and cranny of his creation. After all, the universe is his invention.

TREES HELP US THINK LONG TERM

In the end God declared the condemnations of Job's friends to be wrong and the words of Job to be true. "For you have not spoken of me what is right, as my servant Job has." To underscore this point, God repeated his statement (42:7–8).

There is hope for a tree, and we share this hope. No matter how difficult, painful, and tragic our circumstances, we will see our Redeemer. God certified Job's statements, and the biology of trees bears witness. What followed was both an irony and a stunning exoneration of Job's hope.

As Job was getting ready to declare his belief in God's ability to resurrect him, he longed to have his words of truth remembered. "Oh that my words were written! Oh that they were inscribed in a book!" (19:23). Today, thousands of years later, we study Job's words. The only thing that has lived as long as these lines is (you guessed it) a tree.

Even today, the Bible is the most widely available book on earth. In selecting the metaphor to teach us about resurrection and the timescales of eternity, God chose the one widely dispersed living thing that mimics the promise of life after death: a tree.

Trees live on a different timescale than humans—some live for thousands of years. So does the Bible.

And trees can come back to life after being chopped down. So can humans who embrace the tree of life and the promises of God's living Word.

I don't think it's an accident that as God is trying to teach short-lived humanity about time on a vaster scale, he uses trees. I believe there are two reasons for this: First, trees are the longest-lived creatures on the planet. Second, they are the only creatures that leave a count of every year they have lived.

> I don't think it's an accident that as God is trying to teach short-lived humanity about time on a vaster scale, he uses trees.

At places I have visited, whether Muir Woods in California, Congaree National Park in South Carolina, or the University of Kentucky Arboretum just a few miles from my home, everyone is fascinated by the cross section of a felled ancient tree. Invariably, arrows point to places on the cross section that represent how big the tree was when historical events took place, such as when the Magna Carta was signed, Columbus set sail, or our nation declared its independence. Trees live for vast periods of time; indeed,

God loves them so much that he even presents them with a ring on their birthdays.

TREES KEEP ON GIVING

As I first began uncovering trees in the Bible, God's underlying reason for choosing them to be the workhorse metaphor of Christian life was not immediately apparent. I've come to understand that God chose trees because at every stage of their lives, trees give.

Even in death trees continue to serve. The chances are nearly 100 percent that you've sat on, walked on, or stood under something made of wood in the last sixty minutes. The trees that make this possible are not always noticed. Upholstered sofas and chairs use wood

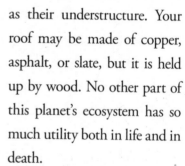

One of the most important reasons God chose trees is because at every stage of their lives, trees give.

as their understructure. Your roof may be made of copper, asphalt, or slate, but it is held up by wood. No other part of this planet's ecosystem has so much utility both in life and in death.

Half of all the creatures on the earth live in or on trees, including trees that are dead. A tree that has fallen in the forest may support several thousand flora and fauna species throughout the course of its decomposition.

To creatures from beavers to woodpeckers, trees represent food and shelter. But to humans they represent something even greater: the promise of life after death.

We do not know what the devil made of Job's fidelity toward God. We do know that God restored the fortunes of Job.

In the end the greatest lesson from Job is a reminder of who our enemy is. It is not the Creator of life and the Giver of trees. Our enemy is the one who thinks we are incapable of loving God simply for who he is, not for what he does for us.

9

Finding Common Ground

On each side of the river stood the tree of life, bearing
twelve crops of fruit, yielding its fruit every month. And
the leaves of the tree are for the healing of the nations.

REVELATION 22:2, NIV

W hat is your favorite tree?" Now, that's a question I love to be
asked. I can't think of a tree I don't want to be beside, under,
or around. But some trees seem to be more perfect to me than others.
And some look their best in a particular light or season.

If you're asking about a specific, one-of-a-kind tree, then the five-
hundred-year-old Cathedral Oak beside the Cathedral of St. John
the Evangelist in Lafayette, Louisiana, comes immediately to mind.
The first branch of this live oak is estimated to weigh more than
140,000 pounds.[4] The Cathedral Oak in Lafayette was in decline
and had stopped putting out flowers. Admirers had compacted the

soil over the tree's roots; they were essentially loving it to death. Then a teenager came to the rescue. He researched the problem and re-landscaped the area beneath the tree's canopy, thereby earning his Eagle Scout standing. The ancient oak is healthy now and ready for the next five hundred years. If you visit the tree, make sure you go into the beautiful cathedral and say a prayer of thanks for the young man who rescued it.

An Ode to Sugar Maples

If you're asking what my favorite species of tree is, then the answer is *Acer saccharum*—the sugar maple. When it comes to sugar maples, it is as if a team of children sat down with God and designed the perfect tree.

"Why are they more perfect than other trees?" you may ask. I'll tell you.

First, sugar maples are as symmetrical as lollipops. Crayon-wielding children draw them by instinct, often placing a round yellow sun and a bird overhead. And birds love sugar maples. As a kid I got to see robins congregating by the dozens in sugar maples.

Which brings me to one of the sugar maple's best qualities: its climb-ability. Even barefoot kids in shorts can shinny up a maple tree. (Try doing that with a cedar!) The maple's bark is smooth, and even in mature trees, the branches persist low to the ground and are well spaced for scaling.

During the summer the leaves display two colors—a dark green on the top and a lighter silvery green underneath. One of my most vivid childhood memories is being up in a sugar maple on a summer afternoon when a thunderstorm suddenly hit. With every gust the tree changed color, inverting the dark green on top for the pale green underneath.

Scientists say the seeds of the sugar maple are designed to fly in order to get them clear of the mother trees' shade. But I believe they were also designed to attract children who like to see how far they can make the bipod seeds helicopter.

Let's not overlook the obvious. The fall color of maple leaves is off the charts. What the sugar maple lacks in springtime in the way of showy flowers, it more than makes up for in its autumn glory. As kids we ironed these harlequin-colored leaves between sheets of waxed paper in an attempt to preserve their beauty. During the summer maple leaves are saturated with green chlorophyll that obscures the vivid colors underneath. It's great to remember that the colors of a maple in the fall have been hiding there all summer long.

One of my best memories is of a fall day when my five-year-old daughter came into the house and hugged me—the smell of the woods and bits of leaves clinging to her hair and wool sweater. If you didn't jump into piles of maple leaves as a child, you should take remedial action.

After I completed medical school and residency, we moved to New England. There I saw what magnificent proportions sugar maples can reach in their preferred northern climate! These were sugar maples on steroids. They grew to four times the size they did in the middle Atlantic region where I grew up. Many were hundreds of years old.

It is not uncommon to come upon one of these ancient trees on the side of a mountain and find an iron plaque affixed, memorializing the passing of a loved one or the date of a marriage a century earlier. One of my favorite plaques is affixed to a lone giant sugar maple at the top of a mountain with a breathtaking view in Chelsea, Vermont.

In New England I became acquainted with one of the most spectacular aspects of sugar maples. During the summer, maples knit carbon dioxide from the air into sugars. The trees bring up water from the soil and make a sugary sap. If the tree were to keep this watery mixture above ground in the winter months, the trees would split as the water expanded when it froze. The trees change their osmotically active sugars to long-chain osmotically inactive starches during the winter months. In sugaring season (usually in March), they convert the starches into sugars again, and this draws groundwater up into the tree, also known as the sap rising or the sap running. The whole system works on turning osmotic gradients on and off. It's quite an ingenious design. Miraculous really.

The sap runs hardest when the nights are cold and the days are sunny and warm. Gathering and processing the sap take constant work. The effort, however, is worth it. Mr. Buttery Syrup Substitute and Aunt June's Gooey Flapjack Goop bear as much similarity to real maple syrup as shaking hands with a stranger does to kissing the one you love. Live on the wild side. Use real maple syrup.

Go ahead and see what air, sun, rain, and wind taste like when a sugar maple gets hold of them. And don't forget to let the children have some real maple syrup on top of snow in the winter.

Planting Trees with Grandchildren

As a small child I tagged along with my father and his father as they planted trees. They made me feel as if I were the one responsible for the saplings' growth, even though I'd only thrown a few small shovelfuls of dirt over the roots and helped with the first watering.

From a faith perspective all parents and grandparents should plant trees with children. It is a tangible way for older folks to say, "We believe in your generation. We don't know what the politics will be in a hundred years or what technologies you will have, but the one thing we are certain about is that you will need trees."

I am grateful that my grandfather spoke the language of trees. Born in 1895, he was a minister's son who graduated from law school before shipping off to France to fight in "the war to end all wars." He got his heel shot off in France, was patched together in England, and went back to the front. Then the index finger on his left hand was shot off. Again, he convalesced in England and was sent back to the front. Then he was gassed and came home to America, blind and deaf. He recovered his sight but not his hearing.

My grandfather went back to school and became a civil engineer, working for the Washington Suburban Sanitary Commission for the rest of his life. He designed places such as Triadelphia Lake and other reservoirs around the nation's capital, which supplied the city with drinking water. Along the way he planted and preserved many a tree. I recall summer picnics by reservoirs and streams, eating and playing under trees he'd protected.

Perhaps the first full-time environmental profession was that of a civil engineer tasked with securing clean drinking water. You can't capture rainwater and use it as drinking water without trees.

With over fifty full-time urban foresters, our nation's capital is a model for protecting its trees and preserving its watersheds. But no city in America is more famous for the development and preservation of its watershed than the Big Apple. If you live in New York City, your tap water is cleaner than what you can buy in a bottle[5]—and it's all thanks to trees, foresters, and civil engineers.

Great Cities Have Great Trees

My grandfather had seen hell on earth. When he came back from the war, he worked to make the earth look a little bit more like heaven. He was proud of the trees of his adopted city.

When I went to medical school in DC, I was lucky enough to live at the north end of Rock Creek Park, the oldest urban park in the country. Although it was created by an act of Congress in 1890, Native American tribes had stewarded the trees for centuries in this watershed, just as modern civil engineers do today.[6] You need trees to prevent floods and make drinking water clean. You need trees to cool a city in summer. You need trees to keep the air clean. Trees act to abate noise in a city. But probably the most important thing trees do for a city is to lift the spirits of its citizens. Trees are a city's stake in its future. Great cities have great trees.

> We can't begin to imagine how beautiful heaven is going to be, but there's one thing we can be sure of: it will be a city filled with trees.

The Bible says that "no eye has seen, nor ear heard, nor the heart of man imagined, what God has prepared for those who love him" (1 Corinthians 2:9). In other words, we can't begin to imagine how beautiful heaven is going to be. One thing we do know: the trees in heaven are going to be out of this world. Imagine the most beautiful tree you've ever seen, and then imagine that you can understand what the tree is actually saying (Psalm 96:12–13). That's heaven!

A Taste of Heaven

This past summer my wife, Nancy, and I got a taste of heaven. We live right downtown in a city of three hundred thousand. The summer is less hectic here because most of the forty-five thousand students and teachers who work and live a few blocks from us take off for the summer. In a stroke of good fortune, the weather turned cool, dry, and breezy—right in the middle of what are usually very hot and humid days. As a result, tens of thousands of air conditioners were turned off. We could open the windows, feel the breeze, and hear!

The quiet we enjoyed was much more profound than even the quiet of a winter day. The reason was the trees. We got to hear what foliage does to urban sound. An average mature shade tree has up to thirty times more square footage in its leafy canopy than it does on the ground under it. The leaves move in the wind and act as acoustical dampeners, softening the sounds of cars and sirens. If you want to get up on your tippy-toes and peek across the divide into heaven, be in a city as it grows still on a cool summer Sunday morning, when no one is rushing off to work.

TREES BIND US TOGETHER

One of the reasons I believe God placed a tree by every important character and event in Scripture is because of trees' nearly universal presence. Trees grow virtually everywhere that humans live on this planet. You may have never seen a sugar maple, just as I have never seen a baobab, but you and I have both seen trees.

I am grateful that people of different faiths as well as people with no faith will be reading this book. Our mutual dependence on trees should bind us together in a common cause—namely, our future. But too often when advocating for creation care, I have encountered opposition from both inside and outside the church. I've met Christians who don't want to work with non-Christians or people from different Christian denominations. Similarly, I've encountered non-

Christians who don't want to work with Christians. As someone who has spent decades on both sides of this equation, I'd like to address this issue.

From a biblical perspective God not only expects us to work with nonbelievers on issues such as water, trees, and the air, but he also models love for nonbelievers and demands that we do the same. When Jesus gave a discourse on love, he reminded his listeners that the Lord cares for all the inhabitants of the world. "I say to you, Love your enemies and pray for those who persecute you, so that you may be sons of your Father who is in heaven. For he makes his sun rise on the evil and on the good, and sends rain on the just and on the unjust" (Matthew 5:44–45).

Yes, it's true. God loves people who don't even believe in him. He sends them rain to grow food and air to breathe. He cares about their well-being. As if to underscore this principle, an entire book of the Bible is devoted to God's love for nonbelievers. Surprisingly, it's one of God's own prophets who objected.

THE RELUCTANT PROPHET

The man who threw a tantrum about God's love for his enemies was one of the mightiest prophets of all. In fact, there is no record of any other prophet preaching to more people or being more successful than Jonah.

Jonah was living in the northern kingdom of Israel when God told him to go to Nineveh, the capital of the Assyrian Empire. He was to tell the people of Nineveh to repent of their evil ways. But Jonah had no interest in helping Israel's enemy. Instead, he went to the port town of Joppa and caught a boat heading in the opposite direction.

While sailing, the ship Jonah was on encountered foul weather. The boat was tossed by the waves, and the sailors jettisoned the cargo and made hurried prayers to their various gods. As everyone prepared to die, Jonah was below deck fast asleep. The crew woke him and implored him to pray to his god. When the storm did not abate, they cast lots to find the one aboard responsible for their misfortune. The lot fell to Jonah. "Who are you, what do you do, where are you from, and who is your god?" they asked.

"I'm a Hebrew, and I worship God, the One who made heaven and earth," Jonah answered. Then he added, with admirable honesty, that he was running from God, and that's why the sea was enraged.

"What can we do to calm the sea?" his fellow travelers asked.

"Throw me overboard," Jonah said. The men were reluctant to take such a drastic measure. But in the end, with giant waves breaking over the deck, they had no choice. They threw Jonah into the sea, and immediately the water grew calm. Jonah was swallowed by a great fish, and the men on board were left astonished and believing in the Lord.

For three days and nights, Jonah was in the belly of the great fish. At last Jonah cried out to the Lord, and the Lord made the great creature vomit Jonah up onto dry land.

Again, the Lord instructed Jonah to go to Nineveh and preach. So Jonah went and proclaimed in the city, "Repent and stop doing evil in the sight of the Lord or in forty days this city will be razed." Amazingly, the people of Nineveh, from the king all the way down to the commoner, repented in sackcloth and ashes, and the entire city, from man to beast, fasted. The Lord accepted their repentance and spared the city his judgment.

Did Jonah celebrate this great success? Did he blog about it? No. Jonah had a hissy fit. "I told everyone you were going to destroy the place, and now I look like a fool," Jonah whined. "You are a loving God, slow to anger and quick to forgive. Just go ahead and kill me. I'd rather be dead than alive."

"Really, Jonah? Don't you think you're overreacting?" the Lord asked.

Then Jonah walked up a hill outside the city and pitched a meager lean-to. He sat in the partial shade as he waited to see if God might yet destroy Nineveh. It was hot in the lean-to, so God made a plant (some translations say "gourd") grow suddenly and shade Jonah, which pleased the prophet and comforted him.

But the next morning God sent a parasite to kill the plant. The sun beat down. "That's it; my plant is dead. I've got no shade. You might as well kill me too!" Jonah wailed.

"Jonah, do you really want to die?" the Lord questioned. "You mourn the loss of a tree that you neither planted nor watered, yet you fail to celebrate the redemption of a city with 120,000 children who don't even know their right hand from their left—not to mention all the innocent animals." On that note of rebuke, the tale of Jonah ends.[7]

What Jonah Teaches Us About God's Nature

Obviously, Jonah made a few mistakes. His first was thinking that he could outrun the Lord. His second was failing to understand that although the people of Nineveh were the enemies of Israel, nonetheless the Lord cared for and loved them. In particular, the Lord has a soft spot for children of this generation and the next and the next. Our myopic view often fails to take into account the past and the future. Yet the Bible teaches a respect for our elders and a concern for the generations to come.

God lives in a timescale of eternity. We dwell in the realm of three score and ten. God is forever trying to get us to think long term, but we resist this with our fallen souls.

One of our problems is that we live such short lives. A human life compared to a mouse's seems long: seventy years versus one. But a human life compared to an ancient tree's is short: seventy years versus five thousand.

God wants us to think more on the scale of trees than of mice. Ultimately, faith in God is about believing we can live, love, and exist on a timescale of eternity. As Proverbs says, "A good man leaves an inheritance to his children's children" (13:22). The Bible enjoins Christians to take the long view and work for the good of the future, even for those who do not believe in God. God is the judge of the earth, not us. Each of us is told to be a witness for God, not the judge, jury, or prosecutor.

> **Christians are instructed to make this earth look more like heaven. Plant trees, care for trees, and preserve old forests. This is a job for believers.**

This does not mean Christians must give up belief in the Bible, God, or an absolute right and wrong. What is certain is that Christians are instructed to make this earth look more like heaven. Plant trees, care for trees, and preserve old forests. This is a job for believers. After all, we are the religion that brings trees into our homes every Christmas as the symbol of our Savior's birth.

What About Working Together?

I recently gave a community talk on trees to a few hundred people at a college in Oregon, and the topic proved to be of great interest to people from many walks of life. In response to one question, I talked at length about ways Christians could do a better job working cooperatively with environmentalists. Believers have a responsibility to steward God's gifts to us—one of which is the earth, God's creation. I mentioned as well that non-Christians could also do a better job of getting along with their Christian neighbors. I cited an essay that is used in college-level environmental studies courses. The writer blames nearly all the world's environmental problems on Western Christendom. Pollution, sunspots, dandruff—everything can be blamed on Christianity according to the sociologist who wrote this article.

"That's not fair, either," I concluded.

> Having plenty of trees on the earth a hundred years from now is in everyone's best interest.

Every one of us acts out of a worldview, whether we acknowledge it or not. Both sides of the tree equation need to accept responsibility, and both need to be respectful.

Very few opinions have ever been changed by starting a conversation with, "You are stupid, and you need to be more like me." Instead, try to find an area of common ground. Having plenty of trees on the earth a hundred years from now is in everyone's best interest.

MAKING THE WORLD A BETTER PLACE

In terms of the environment, we have much to celebrate. When I was in high school, one tributary river of Lake Erie had caught fire on a dozen occasions. Now, thanks to the work of many, you can't even get it to spark. Many of our country's waterways that were not a safe source of drinking water last century are now clean.

When the bald eagle was named our national symbol, there were an estimated one hundred thousand living in the United States. With the widespread use of DDT, their numbers fell to fewer than five hundred nesting pairs by 1963. Since a ban was placed on DDT in the US in 1972, the number of bald eagles has rebounded to nearly ten thousand nesting pairs, according to most recent population figures.[8] Similar rescues from near extinction have been seen in whale populations and other species. We have much to be thankful for and much work yet to do.

Several years ago a group of people got together to plant trees in one of my city's treeless neighborhoods. A group put up the money, and an arborist volunteered to help plant the trees with other volunteers from church and environmental groups. This fall I had occasion to drive down one of the streets where the tree planting took place, and the trees looked lovely. You know what? When I looked at the trees, I couldn't tell whether a Christian or a non-Christian planted them. Only God knows that sort of thing. And he makes the sun shine on all the people and all the trees on the earth.

If you just want to fight, take up boxing. If you want to make the world a better place, go plant trees—even along the streets of Nineveh.

But It's All Going to Burn Anyway . . .

What about Christians who say we don't need to worry about protecting forests because Jesus may return tomorrow? It's true: Jesus said, "Behold, I come quickly" (Revelation 22:12, KJV). I believe him. The end may come tomorrow. Certainly, not a single soul reading this is more than one hundred years away from his personal end time. But failing to care for the earth is risky theological business.

You may ask, "Since the world is in such bad shape, shouldn't we devote all our resources to spreading the gospel?" Indeed, a perusal of the headlines confirms that the world is a mess. If people truly believe the world is coming to an end and pour all their resources into spreading the gospel, I'm all for that. The problem is when we use this as an excuse for doing nothing.

It's one thing to say the Lord is coming quickly and expend all your resources in spreading the gospel. You are on safe biblical ground. But it's quite another thing to say the world is ending soon as an excuse to hoard wealth. I wonder what God thinks about those who wager their grandchildren's futures on bad theology but not their 401(k).

Failing to care for the earth is risky theological business.

Self-serving theology and the hypocrisy that attends it has carried a large number of young people away from the church. They see selfishness and contradictions behind such theology, and they want nothing to do with it. Stewardship of the planet is something God and many young people care deeply about. Respecting God and his creation is something we can all celebrate.

Why Am I on Earth?

Each of us needs to ask, "Why am I on earth?"

I believe God is all-powerful and wants to bring us into relationship with him. I believe this is possible only through Jesus. I believe that my faith in Jesus will someday allow me to live in heaven. So the question is this: If God is all-powerful and wants to bring me to heaven, why wasn't I born in heaven to begin with? Why this life on earth?

Pondering this will likely lead you to the understanding that life is a gift. I'm still taken aback by those who hold that life and the earth aren't worth fighting for. Have they watched snow falling in a forest? Have they stood in the woods at dusk as the stars began to rise? God thought the earth was precious enough to send his only Son to die for it. Shouldn't we be willing to work to make the earth better?

Let's Plant Trees of Life

Life is a gift from God. I, for one, am grateful for it. But I also know that not everyone on the planet has a good life. Nancy and I have cards held by magnets on our refrigerator. They picture the children we support through various relief agencies. One has a portrait of a ten-year-old named Bobby who lives in New Delhi. In his home city air-quality index readings often go over one thousand. For a child like Bobby, this is the equivalent of smoking fifty cigarettes per day. Many problems will have to be addressed to lower the level of air pollution in Bobby's land, but no proposed solution will work without trees.

All over the world, poor people have to deal with a lack of trees. Missionaries working in these places will tell you there is no contradiction between planting trees and planting the gospel. These two tasks go hand in hand, just as they do in the Bible. The tree of life is needed in every form it takes.

When I asked the director of Plant With Purpose (the ministry I donated my book advance to) what his favorite tree was, he said, "I like diversity. I like the trees that give food to children, and clean water to drink." I suppose that in the Creator's eyes all trees are beautiful, but the ones that heal are holy.

> By definition, planting a tree is the only thing you can do in your own backyard that makes the whole world better.

If you think the world is coming to an end, plant a tree.

If you think the world will still be here in a hundred years, plant a tree.

If you want to fight pollution, plant a tree.

By definition, planting a tree is the only thing you can do in your own backyard that makes the whole world better. As Martin Luther is credited with saying, "If I knew the world would end tomorrow, I would still plant a tree."

PART III

Fruit of the Tree

The fruit of the Spirit is love, joy, peace, patience, kindness, goodness, faithfulness, gentleness, self-control; against such things there is no law.

—GALATIANS 5:22–23

10

The Messiah Tree

There shall come forth a shoot from the stump of Jesse,
and a branch from his roots shall bear fruit.

—ISAIAH 11:1

During the summer before I started medical school, I did some carpentry work at the home of a psychiatrist who happened to have a fantastic stereo system.

"Want to hear it?" he asked. He turned on half a dozen switches, and blue-green lights began glowing behind the equipment's glass faceplates.

The good doctor carefully pulled out an album and put a record on the turntable. "I'll just skip the overture," he said as he lowered the needle. There was a moment of silence, and then the sweetest sound I'd ever heard came out of the speakers.

I heard trees and people singing together, and it was perfect. Maples were prominent among the trees represented. But spruce, ebony, willow, boxwood, and rosewood trees sang along too, and none tried to eclipse the others.

"Why does it sound so good?" I asked.

"I think, among other things, it's because they are using a dozen Stradivarius, Guarneri, and Amati instruments, *and* they're performing it the way it was originally played."

We were listening to Handel's *Messiah*—but not just any recording of this famous work. This was by the late Christopher Hogwood and the Academy of Ancient Music. And if you think that trees can't sing, give it a listen.

I bought the album in cassette form, which, to be truthful, didn't sound the same on my Walkman with five-dollar headphones. But it still sounded wonderful.

Throughout medical school I listened to music as I studied. I don't know how many times I listened to the *Messiah*, but it was hundreds and hundreds. Oddly, I never paid attention to the words being sung. It was like someone who hears an aria of Puccini and enjoys it even though he doesn't understand Italian. The sounds and the emotion carry through but not the meaning. That's the way I listened to the *Messiah* for three decades—until the hour I first believed. Then I cried. I sobbed. I wailed. I grinned in delight. And I cried again.

Thousands of people go to churches and symphony halls each year to hear the *Messiah* performed during the Christmas season. Like me, they hear the music and the beauty. Some hear the words and understand. You can spot them. They are the ones blubbering.

I was listening to the best recording of this work, done by the finest artists on the earth, playing the best violins and cellos ever made, and recorded with the best equipment available. I've owned Hogwood's recording on record, cassette, and compact disc. The stringed instruments used by the Academy of Ancient Music were made mostly in northern Italy during the golden age of violin making.

Some postulate that the sweetness, power, and resonance of these instruments can be attributed to the trees used. Perhaps the wood was harvested from trees that grew under climactic stress at the time and had narrower growth rings. Perhaps the trees were harvested in the winter rather than summer. I don't know anything about making violins, but I marvel that something like a maple tree can be used to create something as tough as a bowling lane and as beautiful sounding as a violin. (Scripture records a similar phenomenon in 1 Kings 10:12.)

The music was written by George Frideric Handel, a towering musical genius at the height of his powers. The words were collated by Charles Jennens from a Bible translation the likes of which never had been written before and may never be again: the King James Version. Other than a few words from the Great Bible of 1539 and the translation of the Book of Common Prayer in use at the time, the King James Bible is the sole source of the words used in the *Messiah*. Yet I listened to it for years without hearing the meaning.

Handel's *Messiah* begins, "Comfort ye, comfort ye my people; comfort ye, comfort ye my people." These twelve words take more than a minute to sing. The word *comfort* is stretched out like warm taffy wrapped back and forth on itself, glistening and taking shape. Something otherworldly is at work here.

The words to the first four songs in the *Messiah* come directly from the book of the prophet Isaiah, written 2,700 years ago. I have been a student of the Bible for many years, but my heart nearly fails me when I approach this book. Like Handel, Isaiah stands in a class

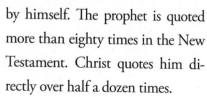

If the Old Testament had a tree nursery in it, it would be found in the book of Isaiah.

by himself. The prophet is quoted more than eighty times in the New Testament. Christ quotes him directly over half a dozen times.

If the Old Testament had a tree nursery in it, it would be found in the book of Isaiah. It is the Grand Central Station of trees. Isaiah's prophecies overflow with trees and metaphors involving the land as they return again and again to describing the coming of the Messiah. That's because the two are connected.

"Look for the Messiah," Isaiah said. "He resembles a tree."

A Prophet's Prophet

The first chapter of Isaiah opens not with prophecy but with Israel being hauled into court by God. The charges against the people are laid out: They are incorrigible teenagers. They think of nothing but themselves. They don't have the sense God gave a donkey (Isaiah 1:2–3).

God is sick of their religious goings-on. He cares nothing for their burnt offerings, solemn assemblies, and pretend devotion. In fact, God is fed up with their religion: "Your new moons and your appointed feasts my soul hates; they have become a burden to me; I am weary of bearing them" (verse 14).

Then God's entire tenor changes, and he proffers one of the most tender invitations in Scripture: "Come now, let us reason together, says the LORD: though your sins are like scarlet, they shall be as white as snow; though they are red like crimson, they shall become like wool" (verse 18).

This whiplash-inducing change in tone from harsh to tender is the hallmark of Isaiah's exquisite writing. It reminds me of the flight of a fly-fishing lure. The lure whips back and forth in ever-changing directions. At any given instant an observer has no idea where the lure might land. But the one fishing knows from the start.

In contrast to this variable tone, Isaiah's knowledge and affection for the natural world are woven steadily through the work from chapter 1 to 66.

BAD NEWS WITH DEFILED GROVES

From chapter 1 onward Isaiah used trees to tell the Hebrew nation good news and bad, starting with the bad. Once again the Hebrew people have gone whoring after idols. Isaiah said they should be ashamed of the oaks and the gardens where they conduct their pagan orgies. Because they perform ceremonies to other gods in these sacred groves ("the oaks that you desired," verse 29), the Hebrew people will wither and be good for nothing but firewood.

In chapter 3 Isaiah prophesied that a nation that forsakes God will no longer have leaders with character or the ability to lead. "I will make boys their princes, and infants shall rule over them. And the people will oppress one another, every one his fellow and every one his neighbor; the youth will be insolent to the elder, and the despised to the honorable" (verses 4–5). While the men of the land will be busy acting like children, Isaiah stated, the women will become haughty and arrogant and adopt lewd fashions, makeup, and hairstyles.

Leaders who act like babies and sport outlandish fashions are not the only consequences that will happen when God's people turn from him. Language will lose its meaning. People will begin to call "evil good and good evil" (5:20), even going so far as calling light dark and darkness light. They will call bitter sweet and vice versa. At times it is hard to tell whether Isaiah is writing about ancient history or the dawn of our current millennium.

Good News Through a Branch

Isaiah also used trees to deliver good news, and the good news was a foolproof method of recognizing the Messiah. "There shall come forth a shoot from the stump of Jesse, and a branch from his roots shall bear fruit" (11:1). By couching his predictions in tree terms, Isaiah pointed out that trees would play a pertinent role in identifying the Messiah. The Messiah would come from the family tree of King David, as David's father was Jesse. Isaiah provided unique details about the Messiah. Hundreds of years later when Jesus arrived, anyone looking for the Messiah could have used these clues to identify him.

If Isaiah had predicted my arrival on the earth, he might have written this: "a male born and raised in Woodfield, had his right thumb amputated and reattached as a teen, worked as a carpenter, married a Jewish woman, became a doctor, had two children, and wrote a book about trees in the Bible." If you know a person well, it's not hard to write an accurate description of his unique identity. But only God can do it ahead of time.

Hundreds of years before it happened, Isaiah narrowed down the possibilities of the man who would fit the description of the Messiah to a field of one. A virgin would conceive the Messiah (7:14). He would be "despised and rejected by men" (53:3). He would be killed for our transgressions (verse 5). He would be led to the slaughter and would make no effort to escape (verse 7). The Messiah would heal the blind and the deaf (35:5). A man from the wilderness would announce the Messiah (40:3–5). And the list goes on . . .

GOD NAILED TO A DEAD TREE

A trip to an art museum might help you understand just how specific and unique Isaiah's predictions about the Messiah were. If you visit a large museum and look at the statues and paintings that depict gods from various times and cultures, you are likely to find artwork that shows animals combined with the bodies of humans.

You will see feathered serpent gods, eagle-headed gods, and fanged gods; some have crowns of gold. If the deities have human forms, they will be magnificent in appearance. Some statues portray gods that have transcended the world with eyes closed in peaceful meditation.

Contrast these images with the most common depiction of the Messiah: Jesus on the cross. Here we see Christ in agony or in death. He has not transcended the sufferings of this world. Quite the opposite: he took on all the world's sin and sorrow. Instead of a crown of gold, he wears a crown of thorns. His clothing is nonexistent, or he is in rags. He is not powerful and looming over humanity; instead, he is nailed to a dead tree.

To quote Isaiah,

> He [the Messiah] grew up before him like a young plant,
>> and like a root out of dry ground;
> he had no form or majesty that we should look at him,
>> and no beauty that we should desire him.
> He was despised and rejected by men,
>> a man of sorrows and acquainted with grief;
> and as one from whom men hide their faces
>> he was despised, and we esteemed him not. (53:2–3)

To stare at a painting of Christ on the cross today is to gaze on a portrait of the Messiah described by Isaiah 2,700 years ago. His likeness is no abstract expressionist rendering. There can be no case of mistaken identity. Isaiah's description resembles only one person in history. Perhaps even more telling, Isaiah's picture of the Messiah resembles no other god in history.

Isaiah was the only prophet to give a physical description of Jesus. Jesus looks as ordinary as a small plant or tree. Unlike the majestic depictions of other gods, nothing is imposing about the appearance of Jesus.

> **Like trees, Jesus gives life. Fallen humanity, however, has a habit of choosing the things that take life away. We reject Jesus, we disobey God, and we walk away from the tree of life.**

And here Isaiah hinted at the reason trees have gone missing from our theology. Like trees, Jesus gives life. Fallen humanity, however, has a habit of choosing the things that take life away. We reject Jesus, we disobey God, and we walk away from the tree of life.

FROM DEATH TO LIFE

One of the Old Testament's most amazing predictions about the Messiah is that he would be resurrected (Psalm 16:10). We discussed this hope of resurrection in previous chapters when we looked at the stories of Isaac and Job. In all these instances—with Isaac, Job, and later with Jesus—resurrection was tied to a tree.

Think about this as you consider the following design challenge: Make a machine one inch by one-quarter inch that contains an internal clock capable of running fifty thousand years. The machine must maintain the integrity of its own software while it is dormant for two thousand years. In two millennia, the machine must be capable of turning itself on. Once activated, the machine must procure the raw materials and power to expand to more than one hundred thousand times its original size and mass, and it may not travel to do this. It must remain stationary. It must be capable of communicating with similar machines regardless of their manufacture date. Lastly, the machine must be capable of supporting human life.

If this sounds impossible, it is not. The machine has already been manufactured and deployed. After two thousand years of dormancy, it is functioning perfectly *and* is currently helping to support human life. This "machine" is a tree.

In the early 1960s archaeologists were excavating the great fortress of Masada in southern Israel, located one thousand feet above the Judaean Desert, when they found a jar containing date seeds. Through carbon dating, the pits were later estimated to be two thousand years old. The date pits were placed in a drawer and left sitting for forty years. Then someone had a brilliant idea: "Why don't we see if these things will sprout?"

A scientist treated the seeds with germination hormones, and one sprouted. The tree that resulted is a male named Methuselah. It now stands more than ten feet tall and is producing pollen. Methuselah has been used to pollinate a female date palm, and the fruit of their crossing has borne children.[9]

Who could have predicted that trees would bounce back to life after two thousand years?

No Trees = Never-Ending Poverty

Years ago I traveled through Honduras on a medical mission trip. I was stunned at the decimation of the landscape that was once a lush forest. The picture is the same in Haiti. It is impossible to effectively address poverty when trees have been subtracted from the landscape. The book of Isaiah describes a barren place being brought back to life:

> When the poor and needy seek water,
>> and there is none,
>> and their tongue is parched with thirst,
> I the Lord will answer them;
>> I the God of Israel will not forsake them.
> I will open rivers on the bare heights,
>> and fountains in the midst of the valleys.
> I will make the wilderness a pool of water,
>> and the dry land springs of water.
> I will put in the wilderness the cedar,
>> the acacia, the myrtle, and the olive.
> I will set in the desert the cypress,
>> the plane and the pine together,
> that they may see and know,
>> may consider and understand together,
> that the hand of the Lord has done this,
>> the Holy One of Israel has created it. (41:17–20)

What a scene God painted: A desert in bloom. Barren land newly covered with cedar, acacia, myrtle, and olive trees. The desert watered and growing cypress, plane, and pine trees. As God says in Isaiah 55:12–13,

> You shall go out in joy
>   and be led forth in peace;
> the mountains and the hills before you
>   shall break forth into singing,
>   and all the trees of the field shall clap their hands.
> Instead of the thorn shall come up the cypress;
>   instead of the brier shall come up the myrtle;
> and it shall make a name for the LORD,
>   an everlasting sign that shall not be cut off.

This scene is being realized in the world today. Since 1979, on one of the largest river islands in the world (Majuli, located in the Brahmaputra River in the northeast corner of India), one man has planted a forest that now totals 1,400 acres.[10] Likewise, the nonprofit I mentioned earlier, Plant With Purpose, has more than two hundred staff members in countries around the world. They are helping to make Isaiah's picture a reality. The trees they plant are lovely in their own right, but one of the greatest benefits of their work is that families stay together. When the land around them supports life, Mom and Dad don't have to travel to a city or another country to find work.

Although many trees are planted and harvested globally each

year, far more are taken down. An area of forest equal to forty foot-ball fields is cut down worldwide every minute.[11] Less than half of the trees are replanted.

WHICH SUPERPOWER WOULD YOU CHOOSE?

Together, my son and I have over fifty years of schooling, two medi-cal doctorates, and four specialty board certifications. There's no nonsense between us when we get to talking. On one occasion we had a very solemn conversation. The topic: Which superpower would we pick if we could have just one?

Flying without having to wait in lines at the airport certainly is appealing. And who would argue with being able to breathe under-water? But my son mentioned one I'd never thought of: the ability to make trees grow as fast as you wanted.

"Think about it, Dad—you could plant mangrove trees and slow down a tsunami. A dense forest could stop an army. There'd be no more hunger. Everyone would have wood for houses and fires."

The rather remarkable thing is that every one of us already pos-sesses a part of this superpower. We can plant and grow trees. We just can't make trees grow instantaneously. Planting, growing, and managing trees happen over a period of time, which forces us to plan ahead if we are to be successful. Trees operate on a timescale that invites us to think long term, which God calls us to do in every area of our lives.

Isaiah frequently looked forward to a time when the Hebrew people would "plant vineyards and eat their fruit . . . for like the days

of a tree shall the days of my people be" (65:21–22). Isaiah was relent-
lessly looking toward a future time of peace. His prediction that
warlike nations would "beat their swords into plowshares" (2:4) was
even made into a sculpture that stands in front of the United Nations
building. It looks forward to a time when God will judge the earth:

> They shall beat their swords into plowshares,
>   and their spears into pruning hooks;
> nation shall not lift up sword against nation,
>   neither shall they learn war anymore. . . .
>
> Sing, O heavens, for the LORD has done it;
>   shout, O depths of the earth;
> break forth into singing, O mountains,
>   O forest, and every tree in it! (2:4; 44:23)

ORCHARDS OF PEACE

Perhaps another reason modern theologians have missed the meaning of trees mentioned in the Bible is that they have never personally
harvested fruit from trees. Not having direct experience picking apples, peaches, or pears, perhaps they fail to realize why Amos, Jeremiah, Isaiah, Micah, Ezekiel, and other prophets made abundant
use of fruit trees as metaphors of God's peace. But they are not just
metaphors.

One of our family's most peaceful memories is harvesting apples.
If you ask me, orchards are as close to heaven as you can get on the

earth. They are beautiful in bloom, in midseason, and at harvest time. Really, is there anything finer than a blooming orchard filled with ecstatic honeybees? No wonder God promised the Hebrew people a land of milk and honey!

I used to take my family to an orchard to pick apples in the fall, and autumn in Maine is the stuff of postcards. The orchard was in New Gloucester, a rural area of the midcoast region, and it sat on a south-facing hillside. The family who ran the orchard ferried pickers and products via horse and wagon. A ten-minute ride put us deep in the heart of the orchard, far from the road. The orchard looked out over the hills and the farms nearby. The quiet in an orchard allows one to hear the birds and the insects that frequent the place.

We often went with another family who had two girls our children's age. After a picnic under the trees, the kids would get to work in earnest. They'd climb up and down the branches, picking Golden Delicious, McIntosh, Macoun, and Cortland apples. My children claim that I never helped with the picking. It is possible that while lying in the grass, a sweater propped under my head, the afternoon sun beating down on my face, I may have fallen asleep. But I was mentally preparing to peel, core, and can their apples. Our bucolic scene was straight from the pages of Isaiah, but at the time I had no clue.

An Endless Forest of Trees

Following Isaiah, the next major prophet on the scene is Jeremiah. The same pattern of trees holds true in the writings of Jeremiah and for the prophets that follow. On the first page of Jeremiah, the prophet says, "The word of the LORD came to me, saying, 'Jeremiah, what do you see?' And I said, 'I see an almond branch.' Then the LORD said to me, 'You have seen well, for I am watching over my word to perform it'" (1:11–12).

Almond trees are the first to flower in spring. Here and throughout the Old Testament, almonds are used to signal God's early and prompt message.

And then comes another famous passage in Jeremiah 17, when God again likens a righteous person to a tree:

> Blessed is the man who trusts in the LORD,
>> whose trust is the LORD.
> He is like a tree planted by water,
>> that sends out its roots by the stream,
> and does not fear when heat comes,
>> for its leaves remain green,
> and is not anxious in the year of drought,
>> for it does not cease to bear fruit. (verses 7–8)

On and on the trees go. The book of Ezekiel is one of the most tree-dense books of the Bible. From the parable of an eagle that lifts up the sprig of a cedar tree in its talon (17:1–10) to the noble cedar that God plants in Israel, the Lord is master of every forest on the earth: "I bring low the high tree, and make high the low tree, dry up the green tree, and make the dry tree flourish" (verse 24).

Another prophet, Daniel, was given a breathtaking vision of heaven. A vast tree at the center gave shelter to birds and shade to beasts and fed all living creatures on the earth (Daniel 4:10–12). Amos cared for sycamore fig trees before God called him to be a prophet (Amos 7:14–15). King Saul met his councilors under a tree (1 Samuel 14:2), and King David was called to battle by God's Spirit in a tree (2 Samuel 5:24). David had a tree branch in his hand when he went up against Goliath, and it's the branch that knocked the giant off his game (1 Samuel 17:40–48). David's ambitious and vain son Absalom was caught in a tree by his hair (2 Samuel 18:9, NLT).

And then came King Solomon, the wisest man who ever lived, who "spoke of trees, from the cedar that is in Lebanon to the hyssop that grows out of the wall" (1 Kings 4:33). Solomon built a forest house (7:2), and Hiram, the king of Tyre, gave him cedars from Lebanon as a gift (5:10). Is there any purer smell than cedarwood *en masse*?

In the Psalms we walk under one tree after another. "The righteous flourish like the palm tree and grow like a cedar in Lebanon. They are planted in the house of the LORD; they flourish in the courts of our God. They still bear fruit in old age; they are ever full of sap and green" (92:12–14). Conversely, God's foes are like "those who swing axes in a forest of trees" (74:5). Your home is blessed when your wife is "like a fruitful vine within your house" and your children are "like olive shoots around your table" (128:3).

I could go on and on with all the trees in the lives of the prophets and kings and in the Wisdom Literature. But I hope you will go and discover some of these groves for yourself.

Pause at the Trees and Ponder Anew

Nearly forty years ago a music-loving psychiatrist introduced me to Isaiah by playing Handel's *Messiah*. Whether his choice of songs was accidental or the hand of providence, I will have to wait to find out. Nonetheless, decades later the seeds he cast sprouted and bloomed. For this I will forever be grateful.

It is my hope that those who read the Bible will pause when they come to one of the thousands of trees I have not included in this survey of the Old Testament. Think about all the good that trees accomplish for our benefit. What a gift from the Lord they are! Listen for the Gardener's voice in the resonance of the Stradivarius and the wail of the Stratocaster. Taste and see that the Lord is good—and so are his trees.

And now, on to the best part of the story: Christ, the true vine.

11

Christ, the True Vine

I am the true vine, and my Father is the vinedresser.
Every branch in me that does not bear fruit he takes
away, and every branch that does bear fruit he prunes,
that it may bear more fruit.

—JOHN 15:1–2

From Jesus's birth in a wooden manger to his death on the cross, the life of the Messiah is inseparable from trees. The entire New Testament is filled with roots, fruit, soils, branches, vines, and seeds. From the opening words of Matthew's gospel describing Jesus's family tree to Revelation's closing image of the tree of life at the center of heaven, we encounter a forest of trees.

Because the language of trees is so prevalent in the story of Christ, in this chapter we will explore some of the major trees that marked Jesus's life, and in the following chapter we will examine Christ's sacrifice on the tree.

Baby Jesus Received "Tree Gifts"

The gospel of Matthew opens with Jesus's family tree. When Jesus was born, wise men from the East arrived in Bethlehem, where they found the newborn King. They offered their gifts of gold, frankincense, and myrrh. The last two gifts are produced from trees—gumlike products harvested from *Boswellia* (frankincense) and *Commiphora* (myrrh) trees.

Have you ever brought a potted plant to a new neighbor? Given a wreath to a friend at Christmastime? Planted a tree at a school ceremony? In doing so, we are following the wise men of old in our giving of "tree gifts" to others.

Right from the beginning and throughout his life, Jesus was never more than a stone's throw from a tree.

Jesus grew up in Nazareth, in the carpentry business of Joseph, his earthly father. There Jesus spent his days among hewn trees, planks, and sawdust. Right from the beginning and throughout his life, Jesus was never more than a stone's throw from a tree.

Jesus Called Nathanael from Under a Fig Tree

After forty days in the wilderness, Jesus began assembling his disciples. Philip, one of the first called, told his friend Nathanael (also referred to as Bartholomew) that he had found the Messiah, "him of whom Moses in the Law and also the prophets wrote, Jesus of Nazareth" (John 1:45).

Nathanael famously responded, "Can anything good come out of Nazareth?" (verse 46). "Come and check it out," Philip urged. As Jesus saw Nathanael approach, he said, "Behold, an Israelite indeed, in whom there is no deceit!" (verse 47). Jesus could just as easily have said, "Behold, an Israel in whom is no Jacob [trickster]." Nathanael certainly got the compliment.

Earlier, Jesus had seen Nathanael under a fig tree (verse 48). The Bible doesn't record what Nathanael was praying at the time Jesus saw him, but the mere mention of the occasion let Nathanael know beyond a shadow of a doubt that Jesus was the Messiah. Perhaps Nathanael had pleaded with the Lord to let him see the Messiah in his lifetime.

But Nathanael, in discounting Nazareth as a worthy hometown for the Messiah, forgot the words of the prophet Isaiah: "He grew up before him like a young plant, and like a root out of dry ground; he had no form or majesty that we should look at him, and no beauty that we should desire him" (53:2). Although we do not know the exact meaning of the name Nazareth, many scholars believe it refers to a little twig. As Isaiah predicted, something great would indeed come out of a town named after a little tree!

Jesus went on to tell Nathanael that he would get to see the ladder Jacob dreamed of long ago: "You will see heaven opened, and the angels of God ascending and descending on the Son of Man"

(John 1:51). In other words, "I (Jesus) am Jacob's ladder." A rescue plan involving trees had been unfolding in time, whether or not Nathanael recognized it.

Jesus Called Zacchaeus Down from a Sycamore Fig

Nathanael is not the only one Jesus called from a tree. In the nineteenth chapter of Luke's gospel, we see Jesus travel to Jericho to rescue a sinner from a tree.

Jericho is a city known for its palms. If by chance your last name is Palmer, someone in your family long ago made a pilgrimage to the Holy Land. People who made pilgrimages to the Holy Land often changed their name to Palmer.[12]

By the time Jesus visited Jericho, the countryside was ablaze with stories of his miracles. Everyone wanted to see him and be seen with him. And in Jericho lived a very wealthy little rascal. He was a Jew no other Jew would claim. His name was Zacchaeus, which means "pure," though he was anything but pure. He was a sellout, a traitor, and a turncoat collaborator with Rome, the overlords of first-century Israel. Worse, he collected taxes. And he was a cheat. His rich clothing, expensive vacations, and lavish estate might have been a small comfort to him.

The Jews looked down on Zacchaeus, and the Romans probably did not think highly of him either. I would guess that he dared not go out at night without his strongmen. At some level of his soul, he wanted to be back in the fold, but it was too late for him.

The one place he most surely avoided was Jerusalem and the temple. No, Zacchaeus stuck to his gated community and his country club. On top of all this, he was a short man, literally looked down on by his fellows. But he'd heard a new rabbi was in the area—a rabbi radically different from any other.

Zacchaeus could no longer go to the temple to make sacrifices for his sins. Being an outcast, he had no place to take his sins. But he had heard that this new rabbi forgave people. No fees, offerings, taxes, or temples were involved.

He desperately wanted to see this man named Jesus. So when Jesus came to town, Zacchaeus ran and shinnied up a sycamore fig tree. As Jesus walked near that tree, hundreds elbowed around him, pressing to get a better view. Jesus looked right up into the fig tree and told Zacchaeus to hurry down. "I must stay at your house today," Jesus said (Luke 19:5).

How much time had passed since a rabbi had spoken to Zacchaeus? The diminutive tax man slid down to ground level. With a look of joy on his face, he took Jesus into his home.

> Zacchaeus shinnied up the tree a sinner and slid down a saint.

The crowd milled about outside, indignant. How could the great rabbi speak to the little traitor—much less eat with him? Sometime later Zacchaeus opened the front gate to his estate, walked out, and faced the crowd. You could almost hear the cameras clicking and the flashes popping and the boom operators working to get the microphones close. Zacchaeus had decided to set things right, including making restitution for the wealth he had gained by cheating people. He said, "Behold, Lord, the half of my goods I give to the poor. And if I have defrauded anyone of anything, I restore it fourfold" (verse 8).

Many in the crowd gasped. Then Jesus said, "Today salvation has come to this house, since he also is a son of Abraham. For the Son of Man came to seek and to save the lost" (verses 9–10).

Zacchaeus shinnied up the tree a sinner and slid down a saint. It's as if Jesus said, "You can no longer hide behind, under, or up a fig tree. I came to save you. I came to set you free."

The Organic Language of Christ

The tree is perhaps the most prevalent metaphor employed by Jesus to warn his listeners.

> Beware of false prophets, who come to you in sheep's clothing but inwardly are ravenous wolves. You will recognize them by their fruits. Are grapes gathered from thornbushes, or figs from thistles? So, every healthy tree bears good fruit, but the diseased tree bears bad fruit. A healthy tree cannot bear bad fruit, nor can a diseased tree bear good fruit. Every tree that does not bear good fruit is cut down and thrown into the fire. Thus you will recognize them by their fruits. (Matthew 7:15–20)

Again in Matthew 12:33, Christ emphatically warned, "Either make the tree good and its fruit good, or make the tree bad and its fruit bad, for the tree is known by its fruit." And he cautioned, "Every plant that my heavenly Father has not planted will be rooted up" (15:13).

The trees that loom large on the first page of the Bible are the working vocabulary of Christ. The thread never stops. To subtract them from Bible commentaries, footnotes, and indexes is to put oneself in direct opposition to the intent of the author of the Bible. When the Word (Jesus) was made flesh and dwelt among people, he used a very exact language. The words he used were organic in their origins—and by this, I mean based in carbon chemistry.

Some scholars in the last century have said that Jesus's language was merely a reflection of the culture around him and that he was employing an easy-to-understand vernacular. There are several good reasons to challenge this.

First, I can find no evidence of Jesus's contemporaries speaking with a similar tone or employing the specific organic language he used. When you read Ovid, Homer, Julius Caesar, and other writers of the ancient world, you will not hear anyone talking in Jesus's consistent and flawless organic language. Further, Jesus's language was precise and accurate, even in areas of knowledge that didn't exist in his time. For example, twenty-four gemstones are mentioned throughout the Bible. Yet Jesus mentioned only one: the pearl. What is unique about the pearl? It is the only gem that is made of organic concretions surrounding an inorganic nidus. In other words, it is the only gemstone that is a hybrid, made from both organic and inorganic material.

Second, Jesus's language was unique in that it did not follow any of the inaccurate thinking common to his day. For example, when

Jesus spoke about the workings of the human body, he did not reference the contemporary beliefs of the first century. There is no mention of the black and yellow bile and the phlegm that were "known" to keep humans alive. The Bible merely says that the life is in the blood. Many centuries later, scientists found that it is, indeed, the blood that circulates oxygen, keeping us alive.

Similarly, Jesus made no mention of the plants that were thought to produce sheep—even though Pliny described such plants in his book *Natural History*. Also missing are Pliny's strange creatures with dog faces or the ones with one enormous foot—the sciapods. Likewise, when Jesus referred to a model of human resurrection, he did not employ what Herodotus, Pliny, or Ovid would have used: the phoenix—an animal they all thought was real. Instead, Jesus used imagery of the tree.

We have only recently confirmed that the tree is a perfect metaphor for resurrection. As I mentioned earlier, a seed from a date palm has been brought back to life after two thousand years of dormancy. The United States has one tree over 4,800 years old. Trees are the oldest living things on the earth and the only flora or fauna known to spring back to life after thousands of years. We know that Jesus was not merely utilizing the simple vernacular of his day, because his speech lacked the errors that were so prevalent in the writings of first-century scholars.

Consider the many errors the Bible does *not* contain. For example, how did the Bible writers know that we think with our brains? Embalmers in ancient Egypt saved the pancreas, bowels, and other organs in canopic jars so that the deceased would have them to think with in the afterlife. Meanwhile, the mummy's brains were tossed in the dustbin.

Yet the Bible, from beginning to end, puts the seat of thinking in the forehead, the brain (Deuteronomy 6:8). That is why observant Jews wear tefillin (small black boxes containing scrolls with verses from the Bible) tied to their foreheads. The author of the Old Testament (God) conveyed the fact that we think with our brains thousands of years before humans made this discovery.

The third, and perhaps most compelling, argument is that if Jesus spoke in the common vernacular, why did his own disciples so often fail to understand him? Why did Jesus find it necessary to spell out the meaning of several of his parables, including the four soils, the weeds and the wheat, and the pearl and the mustard seed? Why did he have to explain these parables to even his closest followers?

When Jesus said, "I am the true vine, and my Father is the vine-dresser" and "By this my Father is glorified, that you bear much fruit and so prove to be my disciples" (John 15:1, 8), he chose his words with exact precision. When we start bringing back this organic language into our scriptural vocabulary, the stories and parables of Jesus become multilayered, like rich humus. They regain their original subtlety and nuances and occasionally even reveal a tone of quiet humor. In short, they convey meaning that we can understand.

JESUS'S BEAUTIFUL TREE PARABLES

We've seen that Jesus was given gifts from trees at birth, that he grew up among trees in Joseph's carpentry shop, and that he called followers from trees. Further, we've been shown that Jesus frequently used trees in his illustrations—and that nothing was casual or accidental about his tree references. He told carpentry jokes about dust and two-by-fours in people's eyes (Matthew 7:3–5). And you might recall that one of the people Jesus healed of blindness saw, at least for a moment, people who resembled walking trees (Mark 8:24).

Christ spoke about the beauty of trees, and he put it in the form of a parable. The word *parable* is Greek in origin, and it means to throw something alongside another thing in order to make a comparison. This is particularly useful when it comes to understanding the relative size of something.

I recently ordered an art book with "over three hundred full-page plates" depicting some of the major works in a museum I had visited. Imagine my surprise when a book less than three inches by three inches arrived. I should have suspected something would be amiss because of the book's low price. But nowhere in the ad for the used book was a size given. Frequently, online sellers of unique or vintage items place a ruler or something of standard dimensions, such as a quarter, beside an item.

Jesus's parables were filled with seeds, trees, branches, and vines.

Positioning one item beside another is perfect for determining relative size. But what scale does one use for justice, compassion, or beauty? That's where parables come in handy.

Jesus's parables were filled with seeds, trees, branches, and vines.

For example, he used a fig tree to illustrate a fruitless life as well as the mercy, grace, and ultimate justice of God:

> A man had a fig tree planted in his vineyard, and he came seeking fruit on it and found none. And he said to the vinedresser, "Look, for three years now I have come seeking fruit on this fig tree, and I find none. Cut it down. Why should it use up the ground?" And he answered him, "Sir, let it alone this year also, until I dig around it and put on manure. Then if it should bear fruit next year, well and good; but if not, you can cut it down." (Luke 13:6–9)

How can we understand the organic language in the parables of Christ when the forest—both in the Bible and on the earth—is vanishing before our eyes?

On the subject of creation, Jesus told a parable about the beauty of what humans create compared to what God creates. In making this comparison, Jesus asked his listeners to call to mind an impressive image—to picture Jerusalem during the reign of its most prestigious ruler, King Solomon.

To gain an idea of the grandeur of something made by humans, let's journey to Jerusalem on a morning almost three thousand years ago. The city was bursting at the seams because on that day a party of foreign dignitaries was visiting the king. Solomon wanted to give them a royal welcome. Thousands of caravans and tents lined the roads leading into the city. Every inn was full. The air was alive with activity. Event planners and protocol ministers had tried to think of everything—but was that possible with so many moving parts?

The king was in his chambers. A dozen tailors and butlers attended him. And this was not just any king. This was the archetype of Plato's philosopher-king. Solomon was a writer and a naturalist without peer. The economy was red hot under his leadership. The entire region was at peace. The roads were safe. Scaffolding and new buildings were everywhere in the capital city.

It had taken several hours to outfit the two thousand chariots with their ceremonial tack, and now they lined every road leading into Jerusalem. Hundreds of men lined up shoulder to shoulder along the last mile into the city, horns of silver in hand, ready to be sounded. The protocol called for the visiting dignitaries to pass the chariots, and when they reached the men with horns, a fanfare would greet their passage as they neared the city walls.

Next in line were government ministers, then Solomon's three hundred concubines. They were followed by the children of the concubines, then the children of the royal wives, and then their mothers—the seven hundred royal-born wives of the king—all of them bathed, perfumed, coifed, and decked out in the finest dresses from their countries. Solomon's first wife, Pharaoh's daughter, was given the most honored spot. The visiting party of dignitaries stopped, and the chorus of Levites then sang the song made famous by Solomon's father, David—a song that millions of people can still recite today: "The Lord Is My Shepherd."

Led by the high priest, the royal visitors took two hours to traverse the last mile. Then, when they were in sight of the temple, the forest palace, and Solomon's palace, three hundred members of the king's personal elite bodyguard marched out in full dress uniforms, each holding a shield made of four pounds of pure gold. They lined up in ranks three deep to the northern side of the courtyard so their shields could catch the light. Just when they grew silent and the guests were bedazzled, two hundred troops, each with an enormous shield made of fifteen pounds of solid gold, marched from the throne hall, through the courtroom, and out into the sun.

With only minutes to go until King Solomon began his procession toward Jotham's upper gate, he was checked by the chief butler, the chief tailor, his minister of state, and his gem steward. No king was ever more elegantly attired. No king ever had a more magnificent court, wives, concubines, children, soldiers, musicians, chariots, advisers, guests of state, or foreign ambassadors. And as Solomon came out into the sun, a roar spread from the thousands in the courtyard, out along the soldiers lining the road, and to the hundreds of thousands who had come to view the spectacle.

Why go into so much detail describing a scene in ancient Jerusalem during the reign of Solomon? Because Jesus asked his listeners to picture this scene, referring to it as "Solomon in all his glory" (Matthew 6:29). Then he threw something alongside this spectacle to give a sense of scale and proportion. He put forth something that outshone the most dazzling king to have ever lived.

What did Jesus throw alongside the glory of King Solomon? One flower. Jesus said that if we can picture Solomon in all his glory and picture a flower beside it, the flower wins. One daisy, one lily of the field, one violet and you've got a picture of something far grander, more elegant, and more sublime than the greatest king who ever lived decked out for a parade of state.

The interesting thing is that just as the tree in its long-lived glory represents the mightiest of all green things, the flower (along with grass) is the Bible's symbol of all that is fleeting and short lived. Read Job 14:1–2, Psalm 103:15–16, Isaiah 5:24, Isaiah 40:6–8, James 1:10, and 1 Peter 1:24 for just a few of the Bible's examples of this. Jesus did not put a cedar of Lebanon, giant sequoia, live oak, Oriental plane, or similar grand tree up against Solomon. Nor did he pit Solomon against the magnolia, weeping cherry, or almond trees in bloom. He used a lowly flower of the field. Jesus explained that his Father cares deeply for these plants. But even in this scale of things, flowers and trees fade to nothing compared to the words of God. "The grass withers, the flower fades, but the word of our God will stand forever" (Isaiah 40:8).

TREES GIVE LIFE; HUMAN CREATIONS END IN DEATH

What if humans had a chance to create their own universe? How would it turn out?

Since humans can't create matter, it might seem a pointless mental exercise to even imagine such a possibility. But in a very real sense, humans have created their own world in the virtual universe. We have created the computer, the internet, and artificial intelligence. God created his world based on carbon chemistry. Humans moved down one notch on the periodic table and created our new world based on the chemistry of silicon.

How is our new silicon world doing? Is it clean, bright, and filled with light? Is it a place without death, disease, or suffering? Is it a place of peace and harmony?

The answer, of course, is that the human-created world is as fallen as the real world, perhaps even more so. It has existed for only a few short decades, yet it has viruses, malware, and Trojan horses. Criminals roam its virtual dark alleys, preying on the weak. Theft is ever present. Addiction is real. People are stalked, bullied, and threatened. Every one of the Ten Commandments has been or can be broken in cyberspace.

How Much Does God Love Trees?

How much does God love the world, including trees and flowers? Enough to send his only Son to die for them. As John the apostle wrote, "God so loved the world, that he gave his only begotten Son, that whosoever believeth in him should not perish, but have everlasting life. For God sent not his Son into the world to condemn the 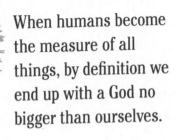 **When humans become the measure of all things, by definition we end up with a God no bigger than ourselves.** world; but that the world through him might be saved" (John 3:16–17, KJV). God loves the whole world, not just the people living in the world. But how much does he love people? Again, let's listen to Jesus.

Have you ever hit a bird while driving? It's an awful feeling. Reflexively, we groan when this happens. We are struck with an instant feeling of loss. The world has just become one sparrow poorer. Interestingly, we are not alone in our reaction. Jesus said, "Not a single sparrow can fall to the ground without your Father knowing it" (Matthew 10:29, NLT).

As you groan when the sparrow hits the windshield, God does too. Jesus went on to tell his listeners that they were worth far more than a sparrow. When we read this passage, most of us jump to thinking about how much God loves us. And he does, in truth, love us more than we can understand. But one of the things Jesus was trying to say is this: "How can you understand how much God loves you if you can't get your head around how much he loves a little sparrow?"

We may value our house, car, or cell phone above all other material things, but that isn't true for God. He is rather fond of birds and trees (Psalm 84:3). He designed the planet so that if there were not birds and bees, flowers and trees, there would be no humans.

Birds and bees, as well as flowers and trees, number among God's greatest tools when he explains how much he loves us. To subtract them from the Bible and our theology diminishes God's ability to communicate his love. It relegates Jesus to the role of afterlife insurance salesman, not the one who sustains all of creation (John 1:3) and for whom all creation was made (Colossians 1:16–17). When humans become the measure of all things, by definition we end up with a God no bigger than ourselves.

Remember when Job and his friends argued about why the world runs the way it does and then God actually showed up? God didn't attempt to explain the world in human terms. Rather, he took Job and his friends on a tour of his creation, from the depths of the ocean to the height of the stars. I think God was not only laying out the university-level science curriculum for the next few thousand years but also challenging us to examine the fruit of our own hands. As he said, "Where were you when I laid the foundation of the earth?" (Job 38:4).

Jesus Sought Refreshment in Olive Groves

Time and again throughout the Gospels, we see Jesus retreat to the wilderness to seek renewal and refreshment. His favorite place to go was a grove atop the Mount of Olives. Jesus went to this beautiful orchard when he was tired, discouraged, frustrated, or downcast.

> When we are tired, when we are discouraged, when we are frustrated, when we are downcast, we need to do what Jesus did: seek solace in the woods.

Whenever the fame and the fury became too oppressive, Jesus found peace speaking to his Father among trees. If Jesus is our teacher, model, and savior, then we should follow his example. When we are tired, when we are discouraged, when we are frustrated, when we are downcast, we need to do what Jesus did: seek solace in the woods.

Go to the forest, sit under the trees, and pray. There, beneath the canopy of shade-giving branches, we, like Jesus, can be still and know God (Psalm 46:10).

12

Christ and the Cross

He himself bore our sins in his body on the tree, that we might die to sin and live to righteousness. By his wounds you have been healed.

—1 Peter 2:24

The last nail fired by the pneumatic nail gun buried itself deep in Tommy Newman's bone. He was holding a two-by-four in place with his toe and knee while his partner nailed the boards. The nails at the bottom of the stud went in as they should, but the one fired up near Tommy's knee encountered a partial void in the doubled-up studs. The nail, looking for something solid to lodge itself in, kept going until it was deep in Tommy's knee. There Tommy stood, nailed to the house.

His friends leaped into action, but framing nails are designed to hold tight. Every attempt to help made Tommy feel like he was being nailed to the house again.

The crew pulled the nails out from the top and bottom plates, freeing Tommy from the house. But his knee was still securely nailed to the eight-foot-long stud and jack (a doubled-up pair of two-by-fours used to hold up a header). Tommy sported two eight-foot-long two-by-four boards nailed to his knee when he arrived at the emergency department.

I was on duty, and my opening gambit to anyone such as Tommy was to introduce myself and say, "I've got more medicine in this hospital than you've got pain." It is amazing how reassuring this is to patients.

Becky, the nurse on duty, was already inserting an IV and asking Tommy if he was allergic to morphine. I couldn't see the head of the nail that had gone into his knee. We grabbed a picture with a portable x-ray.

By good fortune an orthopedic surgeon was in the department putting a cast on a patient, and I showed him the x-ray. "How much of the wood is still attached?" he asked.

"Take a look around the corner," I said.

"He's still got half a house attached to him!" the surgeon said. "Can you get those boards off him and pull the nail here in the ER? I'll take him to the OR and debride the wound afterward." You could see his mind whirling as he tried to solve the problem.

I asked the carpenters if they had any tools with them. They had some in the truck, and I asked for a flat bar, a cat's paw, and two straight claw hammers. I added, "Oh, and a handsaw. I'd prefer a Japanese one that cuts on the pull."

Once the tools were close at hand, I asked the carpenters to help me. I tapped the flat bar between the boards while one of the men held a hammer against the wood on the opposite side. This is an old carpenter's trick. You can drive a nail through a board in midair using it. (It's the same principle as a Newton's cradle, only the mass—or, in this case, the hammer—moves and the board in between remains stationary.)

Thus, we were able to keep Tommy's leg still. In short order I had the two boards separated. Now Tommy was nailed to only one stud. Progress.

The carpenters were wide eyed. I laid the freed stud across the end of a bed and sawed three-quarters of the way through from the top, then turned the saw upside down and finished. This gave me a small square block of wood with no splinters. And yes, I was showing off.

Then I got hold of the nailhead with the hammer's claw and torqued it sideways to start the nail. Next, I put the six-inch block of two-by-four I'd sawed off under the hammer and gently pulled the nail the rest of the way out of Tommy's knee.

"For the love of Mike, where did you learn to handle tools like that?" one of the men asked, awe on his face. I really liked these guys, but I couldn't help myself. With a straight face I replied, "We had to learn it in medical school before they'd let us graduate."

For an instant I could see they thought I was serious. But then I told them I had worked as a carpenter for seven years before going to college. "And truth be told," I said, "medicine is easier than carpentry: if you cut something too short on a person, you can stretch it!"

Jesus the Carpenter, Nailed to a Tree

Doctors are sometimes accused of playing God. Tommy's coworkers at first thought I was more than I seemed because I hid the fact that I'd been a carpenter. Two thousand years ago, a carpenter who was God was nailed to a wooden beam, and it wasn't an accident.

It's hard for me to imagine what was going through the minds of the men who swung the hammers, driving spikes through Jesus's body. The Bible doesn't record their thoughts. We do know that some of the men who were present mocked Jesus and threw dice to see who got his cloak.

The Bible does relate the thoughts of Pilate, the man who sentenced Jesus to death. He was fond of pithy, tweet-sized statements. Here are examples of what Pilate said that day, taken directly from the gospel of John in the Bible:

"What is truth?" (18:38)

"Behold the man!" (19:5)

"What I have written I have written." (19:22)

The statement "Jesus of Nazareth, the King of the Jews" (19:19) was written out, placed on a sign, and nailed above Jesus on the cross. Pilate didn't want anyone to miss this, so he had the sign printed in three languages: Greek, Hebrew, and Latin.

Jesus was far more difficult to kill than people today might realize. He was, after all, 100 percent God and 100 percent human. What do you call that? *Hybrid* hardly seems sufficient. *God in human flesh* captures it.

From the moment he was born, someone was trying to kill Jesus.

Men tried to stab him, stone him, and throw him off a cliff. But it didn't work. He could go forty days without a meal, get into the ring with the toughest opponent on the planet, and walk away after three rounds. There was no point in trying to drown him; he'd walk away from that too. No, the only thing that could kill Jesus was a tree (Galatians 3:13).

And so when they nailed him to a tree, he began to die. The Roman soldiers, the police of the day, beat Jesus's back with a whip before they nailed him to a cross, and they placed a crown of thorns on his head to torture and humiliate him. Jesus's eyes were swollen and bleeding from another game the soldiers played, which involved hitting Jesus in the face while he was blindfolded and asking him to guess who'd done it. In short, Jesus was a bloody mess. He bled from his back, face, and head, not to mention the blood pouring from the nails in his hands and feet.

THREE MEN CALLED FROM A DEAD TREE

On the last day of Christ's life, three men were called from a tree that had its roots, leaves, and branches removed. I'm referring to the cross. The first called was Simon, a man from the city of Cyrene in modern-day Libya. Simon had traveled to Jerusalem to celebrate the Passover and was in the right place at the right time, although at the moment he was first called he might have told you he was in the wrong place at the wrong time.

Simon was on the street in Jerusalem when Jesus, covered in blood and weakened by torture, stumbled as he carried his cross.

"You there, carry the prisoner's cross!" the Roman police commanded. Simon had no choice but to comply. Even though he was dressed in his Passover-go-to-the-temple-best, he took the heavy,

If you have placed your trust in Christ, you, too, have been called from a tree.

blood-soaked cross from the shoulders of Christ and put it on his own shoulders. He helped the Lord of creation carry his burden. Simon's encounter with Christ changed not only his life but also the lives of his whole family. It appears that Simon and his household became early followers of Christ (Mark 15:21; Romans 16:13).

The next person called from the cross was one of the two criminals crucified next to Christ. One of the thieves at Jesus's side mocked Christ. But the other feared God and understood that although he, as a criminal, deserved his sentence, Jesus was innocent. "Jesus, remember me when you come into your kingdom," the thief petitioned. To which Jesus responded, "Truly, I say to you, today you will be with me in paradise" (Luke 23:42–43).

The last person in Scripture called from the cross was one of the soldiers responsible for nailing Jesus to the tree, a Roman centurion. This man ordered—or at the very least condoned—the cruel mocking and torture of Christ. He may very well have been the one who ordered Simon to carry Christ's cross. But he also observed the words and actions of Jesus after he was nailed to the cross. The centurion heard Christ praying for God to forgive his executioners. He saw Jesus ask his best friend to look after his mother. He witnessed Jesus reassuring the thief next to him and heard Jesus proclaim that his work was finished. Finally, he was there when Jesus committed his soul into God's care. The centurion knew Jesus was no ordinary man. He knew Jesus was innocent, saying, "Truly this was the Son of God!" (Matthew 27:54).

Innocent bystander, guilty thief, and cruel soldier—they all were called from the tree. On that day the Roman soldier was the last to be called from a tree. But looking back at the Crucifixion two thousand years later, we can see a more accurate picture. In a very real sense, if you have placed your trust in Christ, you, too, have been called from a tree.

Paradox of the Fig Tree

Despite visiting cities of palms, praying among olive groves, and standing in front of a temple with cedar walls, Jesus never referred directly to any of these trees. With the possible exception of the black mulberry, or sycamine tree (Luke 17:6), Jesus mentioned only one family of trees: the *Ficus,* or fig. In fact, most scholars believe the tree referred to in Luke 17:6 is in the fig family too.

Why did Jesus mention only fig trees? Why was he recorded as having cursed a fig tree and no others (Matthew 21:19)? Why did he use a fig tree to illustrate his three-year ministry to the Jewish people (Luke 13:6–9) as well as to illustrate the coming of the end times (Mark 13:28–31)?

I can think of two reasons. First, Jesus came to act as Jacob's ladder—to be a bridge between heaven and earth, between God and humanity. Adam and Eve hid themselves using fig leaves; thus, the fig became a symbol of the separation between God and man. Jesus came to deal with this symbol and the sin it signifies.

Second, Jesus is not just fully man; he is also fully God. The

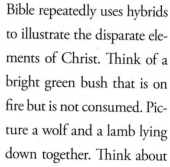

Jesus came to act as Jacob's ladder—to be a bridge between heaven and earth, between God and humanity.

Bible repeatedly uses hybrids to illustrate the disparate elements of Christ. Think of a bright green bush that is on fire but is not consumed. Picture a wolf and a lamb lying down together. Think about God simultaneously being both the Alpha (first) and the Omega (last).

As was mentioned earlier, Jesus referred to only one gem, the pearl. It's no accident that this gem is made naturally of both inorganic and organic material. Indeed, we are told that the gates to heaven are made of this hybrid material. Despite all the jokes about Saint Peter manning the gates, Jesus—fully man and fully God—is the sole gate to heaven.

The mystery of Christ is illustrated by seemingly impossible contrasts: a bush that is burning yet cool; a gentle animal lying down with a predator. Likewise, a fig is unusual in the world of fruits. It is the only fruit that is made of both plant and animal. When you eat a fig, you are not—strictly speaking—eating only fruit but rather a combination of flora and fauna.

When we get an apple with a worm inside, we tend to discard it. But wasps lay their eggs in female figs. When a female wasp finds its way into a female fig (the ones we eat), the fig secretes an enzyme to "digest" the wasp, incorporating it into the fruit. Additionally, the fruit is a collection of the tree's flowers turned inside out. In other words, the flowers of the fig are inside the plant's fruit rather than outside. Just like the pearl, the burning bush, and the wolf and the lamb, the fig is an odd hybrid.

Humans are odd hybrids as well. We ingest poisons (drugs, alcohol) at a level that makes us lose our ability to think straight and causes us to die young. Yet we spend billions of dollars trying to live longer. In an instant we can fly into a rage, and yet we spend decades patiently raising children. We want to live forever, yet we knowingly cut down the lungs of the planet. With the same mouth we curse and praise God.

It is almost as if we are made in the image of God but often resemble a monster at the same time. And that is just what the Bible says we are—kind yet cruel, thoughtful yet unthinking, strong yet weak. To reject the symbolism of the Bible is to reject God's offer of reconciliation. If we do that, the wolf will never lie down with the lamb, the bush will simply burn to ash when it is ablaze, and our fragile bodies will be the only home we ever know.

One more unlikely juxtaposition in the same vein as the others is the combination of dead wood and lamb's blood. In the hybrid world nothing is as powerful as this combination. When the two were combined on a doorway at Passover, the lamb's blood sealed the door shut. The angel of death could not get through such a door, and the people inside were "passed over" and saved.

When the blood of Jesus—the Lamb who takes away the sin of

the world—is spread on the dead tree we call the cross, it, too, becomes a door. But Jesus the carpenter has made a new kind of door
unlike the doorways at the first Passover. It is a narrow door, to be
sure. But the Lamb's blood on it opens the entryway, and heaven is
right behind it.

Although I spent many years learning medicine and carpentry,
which made it possible for me to free Tommy Newman from being
nailed to a piece of wood, there is another part of me—and you—
that would just as soon nail an innocent man to a cross.

WHY DID JESUS HAVE TO DIE ON A TREE?

Still, why a tree? The Romans had many ways to kill people. Why
not burn Jesus in the same way Nero later burned Christ's followers?
Why is a tree the only thing that could kill Jesus? It's because he who
hangs on a tree is cursed (Deuteronomy 21:22–23)—not he who is
stabbed, stoned, thrown off a cliff, or even burned.

But why must Jesus be cursed by God? After all, Jesus was fully
man and fully God. Why did God have to punish God? The Bible
says Jesus came to the earth to pay a debt humanity owed for dis-
obeying God's law. The math of this is beyond me and, I suspect,
beyond all of us.

God set the universe up with immutable laws. Johannes Kepler,
a German mathematician and astronomer, wrote about these laws as
they apply to planetary motion. Boyle and Avogadro wrote about
God's laws of gases. These laws never change. They are immutable.

The laws governing sin are equally immutable. Adam and Eve

were warned that if they ate from the tree of the knowledge of good and evil, they would die. And they did—not immediately, but ultimately and finally. Their death is seen in their separation from God. Even more, they opened the door to mortality for every generation that has followed. This law still governs us today. Despite every advance of modern medicine, no one gets out of this life alive.

In morals, as in math, one side of the equation has to be balanced with the other side. This is called justice. If we fall off a ladder and crash to the ground, we do not question or grow angry with the law of gravity. Gravity is necessary for life and normal human activity.

God's moral laws are the same. We may rail against them when we break them, but when we work within them, life becomes possible. To live under the rule of law is a great blessing—even when we're talking about human laws. To live under the rule of God's laws is divine.

When Adam and Eve broke the only law God had given them, the penalty was death. Yet God has another quality in addition to justice: mercy. In God's mercy he sent his only Son to pay the penalty for humankind's sin. Jesus came to pay a price for every person, from Adam and Eve to you and me and to all who will come after us. Although Jesus was without sin, he came to pay the price for our sin.

The equation of justice and mercy became balanced with the death of a sinless man. I do not understand this, but I accept it. I trust God when it comes to this matter. I have faith in what Jesus said. I know from his teachings that he died for my sins, and I believe his words. When I trust what Jesus taught, the equation becomes balanced.

I have the opportunity and the blessing to live now and forever with my sins forgiven. It is as if my great-great-great-grandparents Adam and Eve never ate from the wrong tree. And it is as if my sins never happened. All we have to do is trust some higher math we can't fully comprehend. Perhaps this is why Jesus said to allow the little children to come to him—because this is how heaven operates. Children can trust what they can't understand.

TRUSTING THE TREE GIVER

A scene from three decades ago will help us identify with deep trust in a father. The event took place behind our home in Vermont, a rural outpost situated at the end of the road. My eighteen-month-old daughter, Emma, and three-year-old son, Clark, played on the floor with Brio trains, blocks, and stuffed animals.

It had been a long, cloudy winter. By February, when this event took place, our town had already gotten twelve feet of snow, and we still had months of winter to go. As I went downstairs to get more firewood, I noted that the pile in the basement was getting low.

"I'll need to go out and transfer some wood into the basement," I said to my wife, Nancy.

"Why don't you take Clark along to help?" she suggested.

Getting a small child into snow gear is like suiting up a Mercury-era astronaut. It would take less time to bring the firewood in from outside than to get Clark into his snowsuit, boots, hat, scarf, and gloves. So I answered, "Great idea."

It was a struggle for me to walk in the deep snow, but at age three, Clark was light enough to simply walk on top. I began clearing a path to the firewood. Once I had the way shoveled, I started transferring wood into the basement.

Our home sat on a steep slope. The ground fell one and a half stories from the front door to the back. A level area by the basement door held stacks of cordwood, and from there the ground fell away in an increasingly steep slope. It terminated in a twenty-foot drop to the frozen road below.

Our kids had been taught to stay well clear of the slope that led to the drop-off. Clark learned never to go where the ground began its steep grade. As I worked bringing wood inside, he played near me. I kept an eye on him, and he stayed where he should.

But there was a problem. The day before, the south-facing area where the slope began had been in the afternoon sun. The surface had melted and refrozen during the night, covering the snow with a slick, invisible crust. Without going past where it was normally safe to play, Clark unwittingly stepped onto the frictionless surface and fell face forward. And because he was on smooth ice, he couldn't get back up the small incline. I was unaware of the situation until I heard him scream, "Dad!"

I turned and saw him sliding toward the cliff. Each time he scrambled to get up, he fell farther down the slope. For a split second he paused and glanced up at me in horror. During that split second his downward slide stopped. In the next instant, when he resumed his attempts to get up, he began sliding downhill again.

"Stop!" I screamed.

I dropped the wood and began running through the snow. As I raced toward Clark, he did the only thing he could do to help. It went against all his natural reflexes, but he stopped moving. He listened to his father. I grabbed him by the hood of his little blue jacket, lifted him up, and hauled him back to safety.

Why did my young son do exactly what he was told? Because he trusted me and because I'd always told him the truth.

When I read the Bible for the first time, one thing that came through to me was that I could trust Jesus. He never lied. He was unaffected by the vanities and failings of the people around him. He had no personal ambition. He had no economic incentives that drove his work. The more famous he became, the less attention he paid to the crowds.

Jesus said he had to be lifted up and hung on a tree, and I believe him. Some believe that science and faith are incompatible. But I think of my faith in Jesus and what happened on the cross as the ultimate science experiment. It takes only one life and the faith of a mustard seed to find out the results. If I'm right and Jesus is the one to be trusted above all else, the reward is great. If I'm wrong, I suspect I'll never know.

When Jesus died on the cross, he balanced an equation. He took the sins of all humankind on himself. The crown of thorns around his head represented the curse of the earth—the thorns and thistles Adam was burdened with in Genesis 3—and this curse was absorbed by Christ.

TREES, LIKE JESUS, GIVE RATHER THAN TAKE

Jesus on the cross is not a pretty sight. Why did God use a tree? I think one reason is that Jesus never took; he only gave. He never owned a house, and the only animal he ever rode was borrowed. He could have dressed like King Solomon, but he is recorded to have owned only one coat.

In many ways trees are like Jesus. They give, and they keep giving. They give life and beauty. They give shade and rest. They make and clean the air. They hold back erosion. They offer shelter, food, and protection.

The worst possible thing to use a tree for is to kill someone. A crucifix is a picture of how low humanity can sink and how far God went to rescue us.

Three days after Jesus was crucified and buried, Mary Magdalene went to the tomb to pay her respects. The tomb was empty. With her eyes burning from crying for days, Mary turned and saw Jesus. But she did not recognize him. She thought he was the gardener (John 20:14–16). This was no mistake. Jesus is the gardener. He is the new Adam (Romans 5:12–18), come to dress and keep the garden, not destroy and plunder it. Adam tore the leaves off the fig. Jesus would not even break a bruised reed (Isaiah 42:3).

> Through the Messiah's death we are offered life. Through his sacrifice our sin is forgiven. None of this works without a tree.

The symbol of Jesus being lifted up on a tree is the only one the Bible offers as a door to the eternal. Jesus said, "I, when I am lifted up from the earth, will draw all people to myself" (John 12:32). Through the Messiah's death we are offered life. Through his sacrifice our sin is forgiven. None of this works without a tree.

13

Christ, the Tree of Life

Blessed are they that do his commandments,
that they may have right to the tree of life.

REVELATION 22:14, KJV

Shortly after I became a Christian, I visited an Augustinian ba-
silica in Rome, Italy. I stood transfixed by a Caravaggio painting
titled *Conversion on the Way to Damascus*. This painting depicts
Saint Paul's trip to Damascus when he fell down blinded and heard
the voice of Jesus (Acts 9:4). In the painting the blinded Paul lies on
his back, arms stretched out helplessly as a horse above him steps
carefully, trying to avoid the thrown rider. The painting is a work of
sublime beauty and searing biblical insight.

No one knows for sure whether Paul was riding a horse when he
was knocked to the ground and heard the voice of the Lord. One
thing is certain, though: God had a special connection to Paul. If
you've seen Jesus, you've seen what God the Father looks like (John

14:9). But if you've seen Paul, you've seen what a fallen man looks like when God gets hold of him.

Before his conversion Paul was an early and zealous persecutor of Christians. He was a member of the tribe of Benjamin and a hotshot scholar who studied under Rabbi Gamaliel. For my Jewish readers, this is the Rabbi Gamaliel mentioned in the Passover Haggadah. Gamaliel's grandfather was the famous Rabbi Hillel after which Hillel houses on college campuses are named.

Not only was Paul one of the chief reasons Christianity spread to the pagan world, but he was also someone sent by God to make early course corrections to the church as it set sail across the oceans of time and culture.

As an academic Paul may not have known which end of a rake to hold, but the gospel was written and designed to go everywhere at every time. So he, too, adopted Christ's organic language and used the tree to explain God's plan.

ROOTS AND BRANCHES OF FAITH

In chapter 11 of Paul's magnificent letter to the Romans, he took up the subject of God's plan for Jews now that Christianity had come onto the scene. Judaism was the root of the tree, and Christians, because of their faith, were branches grafted into this ancient tree. For his illustration Paul used the olive tree. He referred to Jews as the domestic olive and Christians as wild olive branches grafted in.

The branches that were sawed off were thrown aside by God.

These branches represented unbelieving Jews. But Paul warned Christians not to get proud about their newly acquired place on the tree. Never forget, he wrote, that your branch can be taken off, and the old branches can be grafted back in (verses 17–24).

Wild olives grow in Israel, but their fruit is small and of little value compared to their domesticated cousins. When a wild olive branch is grafted into a domesticated olive tree, it produces a plump olive just right for eating. If a wild olive branch is sawed off the domesticated tree and regrafted into a wild olive, its fruit becomes inferior again.

The root of the Christian faith is Judaism. For Christians to ignore or disparage Jews would be to cut off their own roots. It would be as foolish as sitting out on a tree limb while you sawed it off. And Paul challenged us to just watch what happens when one of these original branches believes and is grafted back in (Romans 11:24).

Jesus confirmed Paul's explanation of roots and branches in the book of Revelation. In one of the last lines in the Bible, Jesus said, "I am the root and the descendant of David, the bright morning star" (22:16). This mirrors a preceding line: "I am the Alpha and the Omega, the first and the last, the beginning and the end" (verse 13). Christ is the deepest root of the tree and also the highest branch on its crown. In other words, he said, "I started this, and I finished this."

> Christ is the deepest root of the tree and also the highest branch on its crown.

THE FRUIT OF FRUIT TREES

In his letters Paul also wrote about fruit. When I was in school, the prevailing dictum was that agriculture began with the domestication of wheat and other grasses in the Fertile Crescent. However, cultivated figs have recently been found near Jericho that far predate any evidence of domesticated wheat.[13]

Note that fruit trees are the first identifiable tree in the Bible, and figs precede field crops in Scripture (Genesis 3:7, 18). The starting point of domestic agriculture is not wheat and grains but figs and olives.

Indeed, we can trace a trail of fruit trees that extends from the first pages of the Bible to the last. Joseph was the first fruitful tree we encountered in Genesis. The first psalm tells us to be like a fruit tree. In the New Testament Paul told Gentiles they are grafted into a tree with Jesus. But what kind of fruit does the tree of faith produce?

Paul had something to say on this subject. In his letter to the Galatians, he emphatically wrote that Christ freed us from having to keep all the Jewish laws. But this wasn't so we'd become lawless or subject only to secular laws. Paul wrote that two things are really at the root of our actions: the flesh and the Spirit of God. Which are we ruled by?

The works of the flesh are evident: sexual immorality, impurity, sensuality, idolatry, sorcery, enmity, strife, jealousy, fits of anger, rivalries, dissensions, divisions, envy, drunkenness, orgies, and things like these. I warn you, as I warned you before, that those who do such things will not inherit the kingdom of God. But the fruit of the Spirit is love, joy, peace, patience, kindness, goodness, faithfulness, gentleness, self-control; against such things there is no law. (5:19–23)

Christ did not die on the cross to make sins inconsequential—or worse, to elevate them to the level of a sacrament. He died to free us from our bondage and addiction to sin, including our earthly addictions to wealth, power, and fame. The fruit of our lives should be rooted in the Spirit and not the flesh.

When my lovely wife goes grocery shopping, occasionally I'm allowed to tag along. The first department she encounters is what I call the interactive section. The people shopping in this section do not just grab an item and put it in their carts. No, they interact with the items. This is the produce section, where shoppers inspect, smell, tap, knock, shake, squeeze, and, in the case of grapes, taste the fruit. The Bible tells us to produce the fruit of the Spirit, and it instructs us to test the fruit and make certain it is good (1 Corinthians 11:31).

Perhaps Christians should be squeezing and shaking ourselves to see what kind of fruit we are producing. It would be useful for us to sit down with a notebook and list all the things that make for good fruit of the Spirit according to the writings of Paul. That way we could see how we measure up. How are we doing with our self-control? Are we filled with joy? Or do we get frustrated too easily?

(Guilty!) Is our generosity growing and joyful? Would we give the same amount if we didn't receive a tax deduction?

THE FRAMING SQUARE OF SCRIPTURE

Although it is not cast in tree or carpentry language, I think 1 Corinthians 13 (the Love Chapter) is the framing square of the Bible. It should be used to check the trueness of our faith. Here's what I mean.

I have a power miter box. It is a nice one, with a stand and out-feed and infeed rollers. It can cut a six-inch piece of crown molding set at a forty-five-degree angle against the fence with ease. But all its power and ability come at a cost. Unlike some of the older or less expensive power miter boxes, my fancy whizbang saw comes out of adjustment. When it strays from the correct setting, it still cuts through wood like butter, but the cut pieces aren't of any use. The angles are a degree or two off.

To get the saw back into working order, I have to unplug it, loosen all the stops, get out my forty-year-old aluminum framing square, set the square in the cutting area, and then gently tap the saw until the blade travels smoothly parallel to the framing square.

Our understanding of the Bible is very similar to this. It can come ever so slightly out of alignment. When mine does, I take out a New Testament and reread 1 Corinthians 13. Then I lay it down beside my life to see where I have slipped out of alignment.

If I speak in the tongues of men and of angels, but have not love, I am a noisy gong or a clanging cymbal. And if I have prophetic powers, and understand all mysteries and all knowledge, and if I have all faith, so as to remove mountains, but have not love, I am nothing. If I give away all I have, and if I deliver up my body to be burned, but have not love, I gain nothing.

Love is patient and kind; love does not envy or boast; it is not arrogant or rude. It does not insist on its own way; it is not irritable or resentful; it does not rejoice at wrongdoing, but rejoices with the truth. Love bears all things, believes all things, hopes all things, endures all things.

Love never ends. As for prophecies, they will pass away; as for tongues, they will cease; as for knowledge, it will pass away. For we know in part and we prophesy in part, but when the perfect comes, the partial will pass away. When I was a child, I spoke like a child, I thought like a child, I reasoned like a child. When I became a man, I gave up childish ways. For now we see in a mirror dimly, but then face to face. Now I know in part; then I shall know fully, even as I have been fully known.

So now faith, hope, and love abide, these three; but the greatest of these is love. (verses 1–13)

Faith, knowledge, generosity, and the willingness to sacrifice—these are all good things, but they are not the greatest thing. Love is.

I don't think love was Paul's go-to tool. I think he would have preferred to rely on his intellectual powers or his willingness to be sacrificed. But he knew that God loved the world so much that he sent his Son to save it. So Paul gave the church 1 Corinthians 13 as the framing square to true up our faith.

It's been said that if the only tool you have in your toolbox is a hammer, then the whole world begins to look like a nail. If the only tool you have in the box is love, then the whole world starts to look like it needs to be remodeled, using heaven as the blueprint.

A Love Story

Let me illustrate Paul's framing square with a love story I encountered shortly after I left carpentry. My first job in a hospital was neither glamorous nor high paying. At age twenty-five, I was newly married and just starting my undergraduate studies. To help pay the bills, I worked part time as a security guard at the county hospital.

The hospital was in wild and wonderful West Virginia. My duties included breaking up fights in the emergency department, subduing drunks in the parking lot, and taking bodies to the morgue. Much of my time, however, was spent walking around.

One Saturday while wandering the corridors, I passed a small elderly woman. She sat alone in the windowless waiting room holding a damp handkerchief with her tiny veined hand.

I passed the room several times while making my rounds, and she continued her sad vigil. Hours and hours passed. Eventually, night fell and families went home. Yet she remained.

Something was dreadfully wrong, but what? It is common to see grieving families in a hospital. But they don't sit in waiting rooms for days. When people die, their loved ones leave.

I didn't feel I was in a position to ask a doctor or a nurse for help. So I walked into the unit beside the waiting room and asked the secretary if she knew anything about the woman. The secretary got up, went to the steel button on the wall that operated the heavy door to the unit, depressed it, and went to investigate. She had a short, whispered conversation with the elderly woman in the waiting room.

Moments later, the secretary hurried out and went to the recovery unit, where she approached the nurse caring for an elderly man. A brief exchange followed, and the secretary emerged with an ashen-faced nurse. The two went back through the electric doors and out to the waiting room. They returned, leading the elderly woman.

That morning, the woman's husband had had surgery requiring general anesthesia. His wife had been assured that the surgeon would come by afterward and talk to her. But the surgeon had been called away unexpectedly.

Hour after hour, she waited alone. The anxiety she'd had during her husband's surgery grew, and in time her worst fear—that her husband was dead—seemed to be confirmed. She grieved alone, too timid to ask anyone for information. The day passed. And then they came and got her.

Tears filled her eyes as she was led to her husband. Then she spoke.

"What?" her husband said, lying on his back and unable to see his wife. He couldn't hear much without his hearing aids.

"I thought you were dead!" his wife said, with more volume this time.

"What?"

"I love you!" she cried, handkerchief pressed to her face.

"Oh, Dolly!" he said.

"I love you! I thought I'd lost you!" she shouted.

"Oh, Dolly. I love you too!" he shouted back.

They declared their love for each other at the top of their lungs, oblivious to all who looked on, weeping. The one she loved most had been given back to her. He who was thought dead had been brought back to life.

Imagine for a moment that the person you loved most was declared dead. Hours pass, perhaps even days. And then suddenly that person walks into the room, alive and well. Your response would be euphoric. Jubilant. Ecstatic. Friends you'd never met would cry tears of joy with you.

Paul's framing square reminds us of the Great Commandment: to love God and our neighbors. Jesus told us, "'You shall love the Lord your God with all your heart and with all your soul and with all your mind and with all your strength.' The second is this: 'You shall love your neighbor as yourself.' There is no other commandment greater than these" (Mark 12:30–31).

STEWARDING TREES HELPS US LOVE GOD

We're nearing the end of our journey, so it's time we pulled together the lessons trees teach us and true them up with Paul's framing square. How do trees in Scripture teach us to love God?

Scripture's property law is laid out clearly in Psalm 24:1: "The earth is the LORD's, and everything in it" (NIV).

Records filed at the county courthouse may indicate that we possess an acre or even a thousand acres. But in true biblical terms we own nothing. Everything we own, including every tree on the earth, does not belong to us. Every leaf on every tree, bush, vine, or shrub belongs to God, its creator. As the Bible says, we are but sojourners on this earth (Leviticus 25:23).

> **By planting and caring for trees, we show our loving respect for their rightful owner, the Lord Almighty.**

God has allowed us to be tenants for three score and ten years. But the earth is on loan. We are tasked with passing it on to the next tenants—our children and our children's children—in as good condition as or better condition than we found it.

One of the simplest and most direct ways we can pass along God's good earth in better condition than we received it is to plant trees. By planting and caring for trees, we show our loving respect for their rightful owner, the Lord Almighty.

STEWARDING TREES HELPS US LOVE OUR NEIGHBORS

The second half of the Great Commandment is to love one's neighbors. How do trees help us love our neighbors?

Let's say, for example, that a church or a group of churches de-
cides to partner with residents of a poorer neighborhood to plant
trees along the area's streets. And let's assume that the motivation for
planting trees is the second half of the Great Commandment: to love
our neighbors as ourselves.

Now let's count the ways the simple act of planting trees helps us
express our love for others. Planting trees will produce loving fruit by

- lowering energy costs
- ensuring better water quality
- increasing property values
- reducing crime rates
- producing cleaner air
- providing shade
- creating beauty

Imagine if we also planted fruit orchards in urban empty lots,
planted shade trees around playgrounds, or placed benches under
peaceful groves on our church grounds where anyone would be welcome. The fruit of such practical, hands-on love could be harvested
for generations to come.

God's Throne Faces a Tree

I was once asked on a radio show what I wanted to hear when I got
to heaven. I didn't even have to think for a second. "You're in!" is all
I need to hear.

Like others, I wonder what heaven will be like. On the earth most people place their best chair or couch facing the television. In heaven God's throne faces a tree.

> The angel showed me the river of the water of life, bright as crystal, flowing from the throne of God and of the Lamb through the middle of the street of the city; also, on either side of the river, the tree of life with its twelve kinds of fruit, yielding its fruit each month. The leaves of the tree were for the healing of the nations. (Revelation 22:1–2)

I want to get to heaven to see God. I want to meet the saints. And I want to eat the fruit of heaven.

I grew up on a farm that had a barnyard with peach, pear, and apple trees planted around it. But the best fruit tree of all was the hardest to get to. It was an apple tree that sat in a corner of the field just outside the barnyard. Inside the barnyard, next to the tree, was a large manure pile. The apple tree was in the corner of a field where a tractor couldn't plow, so rocks had been pushed up in the corner and briars had grown up all around the tree.

Jesus described the path to heaven as a narrow road, but I think of the way being like the apple tree in that corner. The best way to access it was to grab on to the fence before you reached the manure pile and then crab-walk sideways along the fence until you reached the tree. Then you'd go up over the fence, avoiding the strand of barbed wire along the top. After all that, you could climb into the big apple tree. The apples were yellow and indescribably sweet.

You may have to climb sideways along a fence over a huge pile of manure. You may have to climb over sharp wire or pick your way through briars. You will certainly have to walk through a wooden doorway covered in Lamb's blood in the shape of a cross. But your goal should be an orchard in heaven.

In a Nutshell

I'm proud of my grown children. But when they were much younger, Clark sometimes teased his little sister. I remember once when Emma was attempting to assemble one of her creations, and she wasn't having any luck. She doggedly kept trying. Clark looked on, seeing her frustration. Then he said, "Emma, you know what?"

She turned toward him, hoping that her big brother would offer advice or lend a helping hand. "What, Clark?" she asked.

"Emma, just remember: if your troubles are many and your triumphs are few, the mighty oak was once a little nut like you."

Trees are the only things from our childhood that are bigger when we go back and visit them as adults. Our faith should be like that.

Clark was giving his sister a hard time, but his words held more than a kernel of truth. No one ever sees a tree grow. It starts as a little seed or nut that has fallen to the ground. It carries a germ of energy from the tree it fell from, but it must leaf out and reach for the light. It goes through seasons and weathers storms. Eventually it stands tall.

Trees are the only things from our childhood that are bigger when we go back and visit them as adults. Our faith should be like that. The Bible doesn't tell us to be like a house or a chariot or a lion. It tells us to be like a fruitful tree. Grow, make the world better, and bear fruit.

Epilogue

Bringing Heaven to Earth

Thy kingdom come, Thy will be done in earth,

as it is in heaven.

—THE LORD'S PRAYER (MATTHEW 6:10, KJV)

O n a morning in March 1867 in the city of Indianapolis, John, an inventor in his midtwenties, was crouched down, trying to get the drive belt off a large machine. He was a diligent worker, so rather than asking for help or stopping to get a different tool, he used the sharp back end of a file to work at freeing the belt from the equipment.

As he tugged, the file slipped and the pointed end buried itself deep in the globe of his eye. He stood holding his hand to his punctured eye as the fluid drained into his palm. "My right eye is gone!" he cried.

By the time he could be examined by a doctor, John was unable to see out of both eyes. The doctor prescribed convalescence in a darkened room. John feared that his eyesight was "closed forever on all God's beauty." Can you imagine his despair? He vowed to God that if he ever recovered his sight, he would no longer spend his time inventing industrial items but would instead ponder the "inventions of God" that could be seen only in the outdoors.[14]

Even before his eye was injured, John was a remarkable man. He was once asked about getting patents on his inventions. He answered, "I believe all improvements and inventions should be the property of the human race. No inventor has the right to profit by an invention for which he deserves no credit. The idea of it was really inspired by the Almighty."[15]

Miraculously, after a month John Muir recovered his sight in both eyes. "God has nearly to kill us sometimes, to teach us lessons," he exclaimed.[16] True to his vow, Muir never returned to factory life. America and the world are forever richer because of his decision.

Muir was a man of deep faith. Everywhere in nature, he saw God's wonder and handiwork. His writing and language mirror that of the Bible, of which he is said to have memorized the entire New Testament.

We get a glimpse into Muir's faith in an incident that occurred when he traveled across the war-torn South two years after the close of the Civil War. He walked a thousand miles from Louisville, Kentucky, to the coast of Florida.

On one occasion a man took Muir's backpack with all his possessions. When the robber looked in the pack, he found only a comb, a brush, a towel, soap, a change of underclothing, a copy of Robert

Burns's poems, John Milton's *Paradise Lost,* and a small New Testament. The thief gave the pack and all its contents back to Muir.[17]

Can you imagine traversing the southeastern United States on foot with so little? Muir carried fewer than a dozen items, and one of them was a New Testament. One of the other books, *Paradise Lost,* was about God too. Scripture provided the foundations for Muir's life's work.

Over the next four decades, Muir became a writer and a naturalist without peer. He and President Teddy Roosevelt famously camped alone in Yosemite Valley in 1903. Their conversation around the campfire marked the beginning of a great national park movement—not only in the United States but also around the globe.[18] I believe God used Muir to save more trees and wilderness than any person in history.

As Tertullian put it around the year 200, "Nature is school-mistress, the soul the pupil; and whatever one has taught or the other has learned has come from God—the Teacher of the teacher."

God's "invisible attributes, namely, his eternal power and divine nature, have been clearly perceived, ever since the creation of the world, in the things that have been made." This quote about God and nature goes on to say that people are "without excuse" if they claim not to know there is a God after going for a walk in the woods.

However much this thinking might sound like Muir's writing, he did not pen it. It comes from the Bible (Romans 1:20) and reflects the orthodox thinking of Christians in every generation from the first century onward. Or, as Tertullian put it around the year 200, "Nature is school-mistress, the soul the pupil; and whatever one has taught or the other has learned has come from God—the Teacher of the teacher."[19]

SAINT FRANCIS AND SAN FRANCISCO

A decade ago I traveled to San Francisco to accept an honor from the Sierra Club. Beforehand, Nancy and I visited Muir Woods just north of the city. I have preached about God from the pulpit of the Washington National Cathedral on several occasions. But when we stood in silence, dwarfed by towering old-growth redwoods of the Cathedral Grove in Muir Woods, God did the teaching.

The following day I met with the board of the Sierra Club. Although some there did not share my belief in God, we all had a fondness for his trees.

They listened to the things I wanted to share, and I answered what I could of their questions. At the end of our discussion, I said, "How can I be in the city named after the patron saint of the environment and not say his prayer? Will those of you who believe in God please bow your head and pray with me, and will those of you who don't please close your eyes and pray *for* me?"

Everyone stood and bowed their heads as we prayed,

Lord, make me an instrument of your peace:
where there is hatred, let me sow love;
where there is injury, pardon;
where there is doubt, faith;
where there is despair, hope;
where there is darkness, light;
where there is sadness, joy.

O divine Master, grant that I may not so much seek
to be consoled as to console,
to be understood as to understand,
to be loved as to love.
For it is in giving that we receive,
it is in pardoning that we are pardoned,
and it is in dying that we are born to eternal life.
Amen.[20]

Why I Wrote This Book

My hope in writing this book is twofold: first, to begin a conversation and, second, to inspire people toward action.

First, the conversation. Dozens of books have been published on forests and on the nomenclature, genetics, physiology, and ecosystems of trees. Many colorful books describe the beauty of trees. But only the Bible tells us about God and trees.

God's original plan was for humanity to dress and keep trees. For those of us who claim the name of Christ, we ought to take a long, hard look at how well we are fulfilling our role as God's stewards.

There are two trees of life (*etz chayim*, Hebrew for "tree of life"):[21] the biological trees God created to give oxygen to every creature on the earth, and the wisdom of the Bible, which offers eternal life.

How well are we stewarding the trees? Are we taking care of God's forests? Are we being responsible or foolish stewards? We also need to question how well we are protecting God's Word. Have we taken trees out of our theology? It has been said that everything important in life takes place between three trees—the tree in Eden, the tree on Calvary, and the tree in heaven. When we fail to take note of these trees, we risk losing the gospel. And when we lose the gospel, we lose hope.

For those who do not know Jesus, I pray this book offers a ray of light into the hope of Christ. Read the Bible with an open heart. Follow the trail of trees. Then ask God to graft you into his Tree of Life. You can do this underneath a tree. As this book chronicles, it's worked for many before.

Perhaps you have wandered away from the church. In college you might have been presented with a false dichotomy: science or religion, empirical knowledge or unthinking faith. Or perhaps at some point in your past you were hurt by a Christian friend or relative—maybe one who, out of ignorance, told you God does not care about creation. For this please accept my humblest and sincerest apologies. But don't throw the baby out with the bathwater. I had a few bad teachers in school, but that does not mean that an education isn't a great thing.

I invite believers and nonbelievers alike to examine the Bible, paying attention to the trees that populate Scripture. You will be rewarded with a deeper understanding of the gospel as well as a greater respect for God's second book, his creation.

The second reason I wrote this book is to inspire people toward action. I spent several days speaking at Southeastern Baptist Theological Seminary in Wake Forest, North Carolina. In addition to speaking at chapel services, in the classroom, and at a community event, I gave a talk on trees and Scripture. The talk was all theology and no application. A professor came up to me afterward and asked, "But what can we do?"

The statistics on how many acres of forest are lost worldwide each year are difficult to fathom. But you can do something about it. Like Abraham, you can plant trees. With the purchase of this book, .

you have already begun through a donation to Plant With Purpose. Visit our website, BlessedEarth.org, for a list of ideas to get you started. Then drop me a line at matthew@blessedearth.org to let me know what you are doing.

Together, we can reforest faith!

Notes

1. "The World's 8 Richest Men Are Now as Wealthy as Half the World's Population," *Forbes,* January 16, 2017, http://fortune.com/2017/01/16/world-richest-men-income-equality/.
2. Doreen Ajiambo, "Witch Doctors Sacrificing Children in This Drought-Stricken African Country," *USA Today,* September 26, 2017, www.usatoday.com/story/news/world/2017/09/26/witch-doctors-sacrificing-children-drought-stricken-african-country-uganda/703756001/.
3. Richard Grant, "Do Trees Talk to Each Other?" *Smithsonian Magazine,* March 2018, www.smithsonianmag.com/science-nature/the-whispering-trees-180968084/.
4. From the plaque in front of the St. John Cathedral Oak, Lafayette, Louisiana.
5. New York City Environmental Protection, "Drinking Water," www.nyc.gov/html/dep/html/drinking_water/index.shtml.
6. National Park Service, "History and Culture," Rock Creek, www.nps.gov/rocr/learn/historyculture/index.htm.
7. Jonah 1–4, paraphrased by author.
8. "Fact Sheet: Natural History, Ecology, and History of Recovery," US Fish and Wildlife Service, June 2007, www.fws.gov/midwest/eagle/recovery/biologue.html.

9. Ed Yong, "2,000 Year Old 'Phoenix' Seed Rises from the Ashes," *National Geographic,* June 12, 2008, www.national geographic.com/science/phenomena/2008/06/12/2000-year -old-phoenix-seed-rises-from-the-ashes/.

10. Zi-Ann Lum, "One Man Single-Handedly Plants Forest Bigger Than Central Park," *Huffington Post,* October 28, 2014, www .huffingtonpost.ca/2014/10/28/jadav-payeng-forest-man-majuli _n_6026242.html.

11. "The World Lost 40 Football Fields of Tropical Trees Every Minute in 2017," *E360 Digest,* Yale School of Forestry and Environmental Studies, June 27, 2018, https://e360.yale.edu /digest/the-world-lost-40-football-fields-of-tropical-trees-every -minute-in-2017.

12. "Palmer History, Family Crest, and Coat of Arms," House of Names.com, www.houseofnames.com/palmer-family-crest.

13. Steve Bradt, "Figs Likely First Domesticated Crop," *The Harvard Gazette,* June 8, 2006, https://news.harvard.edu/gazette /story/2006/06/figs-likely-first-domesticated-crop/.

14. Tom Melham, *John Muir's Wild America* (Washington, DC: National Geographic Society, 1976), 40, 44.

15. Linnie Marsh Wolfe, *Son of the Wilderness: The Life of John Muir* (New York: Alfred A. Knopf, 1945; Madison: University of Wisconsin Press, 2003), 99.

16. Melham, *John Muir's Wild America,* 44.

17. Melham, *John Muir's Wild America,* 48–49.

18. Wolfe, *Son of the Wilderness,* 291–94.

19. Tertullian, quoted in Ralph L. Woods, ed., *The World Treasury of Religious Quotations* (New York: Garland Books, 1966), 675.

20. "Peace Prayer of Saint Francis," Loyola Press, www.loyolapress.com/our-catholic-faith/prayer/traditional-catholic-prayers/saints-prayers/peace-prayer-of-saint-francis.

21. John J. Parsons, "Etz Chayim: Tree of Life," Hebrew for Christians, https://hebrew4christians.com/Meditations/Etz_Chaim/etz_chaim.html.

About the Author

Matthew Sleeth, MD, a former emergency room physician and chief of hospital medical staff, resigned from his position to teach, preach, and write about faith and stewardship issues. Dr. Sleeth has spoken at more than one thousand churches, campuses, and events, including serving as a monthly guest preacher at the Washington National Cathedral. Recognized by *Newsweek* as one of the nation's most influential Christian leaders, Dr. Sleeth is the executive director of Blessed Earth and author of numerous articles and books, including *Serve God, Save the Planet* and *24/6*. He lives in Lexington, Kentucky, with Nancy, his wife of nearly forty years. Their grown children serve with their spouses in full-time parish ministry and as medical missionaries in Africa.

About Blessed Earth

Blessed Earth is an educational nonprofit founded by Matthew and Nancy Sleeth. The mission of Blessed Earth is to inspire faithful stewardship of all creation. Please visit the Blessed Earth website for creation care and tree scriptures, hymns, sermon outlines, articles, films, books, and additional resources.